Cooking with the Wines of

Oregon

Cooking with the Wines of

Oregon

TROY & CHERYL-LYNN TOWNSIN

whitecap

Edited by Elaine Jones
Proofread by Lesley Cameron
Design by Michelle Mayne
Food photography by Tracey Kusiewicz

Regional Oregon winery maps from the *Holiday Guide to Oregon Wineries*, published
November 14, 2006, © 2006 *The Oregonian*. All rights reserved. Reprinted with permission.

Printed in Canada by Friesens

LIBRARY AND ARCHIVES CANADA CATALOGUING IN PUBLICATION

Townsin, Troy, 1975–
        Cooking with the wines of Oregon / Troy Townsin, Cheryl-Lynn Townsin.

Includes index.
ISBN-13: 978-1-55285-843-1
ISBN-10: 1-55285-843-X

1. Cookery (Wine). 2. Wine and wine making--Oregon. 3. Wineries--Oregon.
I. Townsin, Cheryl-Lynn, 1979– II. Title.

TX726.T694 2007   641.6'22   C2006-904989-0

The publisher acknowledges the financial support of the Government of Canada through
the Book Publishing Industry Development Program (BPIDP) and the Province of British
Columbia through the Book Publishing Tax Credit.

HOW CAN WE IMPROVE?

We strive for excellence and we value any feedback that will help make our books better.
We'd love to hear your suggestions, and if you come across information that's out of date
we'd appreciate you letting us know so we can amend future editions. And feel free to tell
us which recipes you like so we can keep the book chock-full of your favorites. You can
email us at contactus@polyglotpublishing.com.

PROP SOURCES

Tools & Techniques Ltd.
250–16th Street West
Vancouver B.C. V7V 3R5
604-925-1835
www.thestoreforcooks.com

The Gourmet Warehouse
1340 East Hastings
Vancouver B.C. V5L 1S3
604-253-3022
www.gourmetwarehouse.ca

Pottery Barn
2600 Granville Street
Vancouver B.C.
604-678-9897
www.potterybarn.ca

Chintz & Co.
950 Homer Street
Vancouver B.C. V6B 2W7
604-689-2022
www.chintz.com

Contents

Introduction

OREGON STATE IS HOME TO SOME OF THE WORLD'S FINEST
wines. From the rolling foothills of volcanic Mount Hood
through the bustling city of Portland, heading east through
the Columbia Gorge and Columbia Valley to the Walla Walla
Valley, back down past historic Salem and Eugene through
the forested valleys of the Umpqua, to the banks of the
mighty Rogue River and along its many tributaries, there
are vineyards rich with grapes just waiting to be turned into
incredible wines that will win accolades from consumers and
wine judges the world over.

This book pays tribute to the wineries of Oregon with
a collection of 100 recipes for cooking with wine. Many
of the recipes come directly from the wineries—some are
family secrets being published here for the first time. Others
are adaptations of old classics, and a number were created
by world-renowned chefs especially for this book. All of the
recipes have been tried and tested, and we're sure you'll
enjoy them.

Cooking with wine can make the difference between a
good meal and a great meal. But don't forget the golden rule:
you must never cook with a wine you wouldn't drink. Never
use anything labeled "cooking wine," as these awful concoctions
are full of vinegar or salt and can ruin a perfectly good meal.

You may be surprised to learn that cooking with wine also
has certain health benefits. Studies show not only that wine is
beneficial for the heart, but also that cooking with wine helps
reduce salt intake by increasing the flavor of food. Do your
health a favor and include a little wine in your cooking!

Don't worry too much about the alcohol content of the
wine you use in cooking. When wine is heated, the alcohol
is significantly reduced. However, it would require a lot of
cooking time to completely remove the alcohol, so if someone
can't consume any alcohol, it's safer not to serve him or her
food cooked with wine. As you work your way through the

recipes in this book, you'll discover that cooking with wine is not only easy, it's also a fun, rewarding and social experience.

We're often asked about pairing wine and food. Cooking with wine can be the answer to all your "pairing" problems. When we match wines with foods, we try to find flavors in the food that complement the flavors in the wine. Cooking with wine infuses the food with the flavors of the wine. If you serve the same wine with your meal, you'll have a perfect match nearly every time.

Oregon is abundant in magnificent fresh produce, and we wholeheartedly believe in using local ingredients when preparing meals. Oregon's hazelnuts are sought-after around the globe, and big, juicy marionberries are an Oregon specialty that visitors to the state will talk about years after their visit. Vine-ripened tomatoes, broccoli, beets, wild mushrooms, corn, melons, spinach, beans, squash, peppers, pumpkins, cherries, apples and pears are only a fraction of what is grown in the fertile soil of this state.

Its Pacific coastline gives Oregon the world's finest Dungeness crab, wild salmon, succulent oysters, razor clams, trout, mussels and other varieties of fish and shellfish. Home-grown lamb, organic beef and free-range chicken can be found in the markets, as well as farm-raised venison, goat, rabbit and quail. There are artisanal cheeses, smokehouse meats and heavenly handmade chocolates, for which Oregon is famous.

With all this natural abundance it's not surprising that Oregon's wine industry is also known for its excellence, and its flagship is without a doubt Pinot Noir. Each summer, the International Pinot Noir Celebration is held in McMinnville, where the world's best Pinot Noirs are poured alongside Oregon's finest. Each year, Oregon's Pinot Noir awes wine critics from around the globe. Oregon winemakers are also wowing the wine world with their lively Pinot Gris, fresh Rieslings, elegant Chardonnays, bold Cabernet Sauvignons and

COOKING CONVERSION CHARTS

Imperial	Metric
¼ tsp	1 mL
½ tsp	2 mL
1 tsp	5 mL
2 tsp	10 mL
1 Tbsp	15 mL
2 Tbsp	25 mL
¼ cup	50 mL
⅓ cup	75 mL
½ cup	125 mL
⅔ cup	150 mL
¾ cup	175 mL
1 cup	250 mL

Imperial		Metric
oz	lb	
¼ oz	–	7 gm
½ oz	–	15 gm
1 oz	–	30 gm
2 oz	–	55 gm
4 oz	¼ lb	110 gm
5 oz	–	140 gm
8 oz	½ lb	230 gm
10 oz	–	280 gm
16 oz	1 lb	450 gm
24 oz	1½ lb	680 gm
32 oz	2 lb	900 gm

cherry red Merlots. In all, more than 40 types of wine grapes grow in the state, including some lesser-known varietals, such as Tempranillo, Maréchal Foch, Barbera, Müller Thurgau and Early Muscat.

In this book we've tried to include recipes that cater to as wide a variety of tastes as possible, although it's only fair to warn you that we do love garlic. If there's too much garlic in a recipe for your liking, feel free to tone it down. The same goes for any other ingredients you either don't have or don't want to use. The recipes are guides for your own culinary adventures, and it's often fun to experiment and substitute.

The most important thing to remember when cooking for others is that your guests are there to spend time with you. Do as much preparation as you possibly can before they arrive so you can enjoy their company. This is every bit as important as good food and good wine. Pour some wine and invite your guests into the kitchen while you finish making the meal. Make cooking a time to socialize and have fun.

You have the ingredients and you have the wine. This book was created to help you bring the two together. It's full of inspired dishes that often combine unusual yet wonderful flavors and textures. There are simple-to-prepare dishes that you can whip up after work using what you have in the pantry, and there are exquisite, more time-consuming recipes for special occasions.

If there is wine terminology you're unfamiliar with, don't be afraid to ask about it at the wineries or your local wine store. Wine lovers are usually thrilled when they get a chance to discuss their passion with someone who is interested.

In addition to being a cookbook, this is a guide to all of Oregon's magnificent wineries, making touring a little easier and more enjoyable. You will find a listing, by area, of all Oregon's wineries, complete with maps, beginning on page 198. So get out there and enjoy Oregon's spectacular scenery, visit the wineries, then grab a corkscrew and a bottle of your favorite wine and use this book to cook yourself up an unforgettable feast.

Fahrenheit	Celsius
175	80
200	95
225	110
250	120
275	140
300	150
325	160
350	180
375	190
400	200
425	220
450	230

Appetizers

God in his goodness sent the grapes, to cheer both great and small.
Little fools will drink too much, and great fools not at all.

—Anonymous

Woolridge Creek Grilled Zucchini and Prosciutto Shrimp

featuring WOOLRIDGE CREEK WARRICK WHITE

2 Tbsp olive oil

¼ cup white wine

3 Tbsp fresh lemon juice

1 tsp fresh thyme

2 cloves garlic, crushed

1 lb raw shrimp, peeled and deveined

¼ cup basil oil (optional—Consorzio is very good)

2 Tbsp chopped lemon zest (optional)

1 lb zucchini, sliced diagonally

salt and freshly ground black pepper to taste

6-8 slices prosciutto, cut into strips

Kara Olmo of Woolridge Creek created this summertime grilled appetizer. The wine is a rich, full, fruity blend of Chardonnay, Pinot Noir and Viognier that pairs magnificently with this gourmet opener for your dinner.

1. Combine 1 Tbsp of the olive oil with the wine, lemon juice, thyme and garlic in a bowl. Add the shrimp and marinate for 30 minutes. If using, combine the basil oil and lemon zest in a separate small bowl and let it stand for at least 30 minutes.

2. Preheat the grill to medium-high. Lightly oil, salt and pepper the sliced zucchini and grill for 5–7 minutes. Place the shrimp on skewers and grill for 5–7 minutes. (If you're using wooden skewers, presoak them in water for 30 minutes so they don't burn.)

3. Wrap each grilled shrimp in prosciutto and place on a grilled slice of zucchini. If using the lemon-basil oil, drizzle it overtop. Serve with a glass of Warrick White.

SERVES 4–6

WOOLRIDGE CREEK WINERY AND
VINEYARD
818 Slagle Creek Road, Grants Pass
TEL: (541) 846-6364 or
1 (800) 863-5675
www.wcwinery.com
admin@wcwinery.com

WINE SHOP, TOURS AND TASTINGS
Open weekends 11 a.m.–5 p.m. or by
appointment.

GETTING THERE
From I-5 at Grants Pass take US-199
to Oregon Caves/Crescent City, exit
55 and go ½ mile. Continue onto
Grants Pass Parkway and then bear
right at Redwood Highway. Turn left
at Williams Highway/Highway 238
and follow for 6 miles. Turn left at
North Applegate Road and go
7 miles. Turn left at Kubli Road, then
turn right onto Slagle Creek Road.

WINERY HIGHLIGHTS
In the summer there are panoramic
views and outdoor patios; an open
fire is usually going indoors when
it's cool.

AVA

*AVA stands for American Viticultural Area. These
areas, or appellations, are designated and administered
by the Alcohol Tobacco Tax and Trade Bureau (TTB).
The system of AVAs is roughly based on the French
system of* **Appellation d'Origine Contrôlée (AOC)**
with one huge difference.

*AVAs are geographic boundaries only. The French
appellation system offers a lot more information about
what you can expect to find inside a bottle of wine.
The French AOC system provides information such as
maximum yields, minimum sugar levels, time in oak,
whether or not sugar has been added and more. In the
United States, we are only given the broad geographic
region where the grapes have been grown. The TTB
has defined AVAs as "a delimited grape-growing region
distinguishable by geographic features." These features
refer to soil content, climate and general growing
conditions that make the area unique.*

*There are around 100 AVAs in California alone and
more are being recognized each year. In Oregon (at
the time of going to print), the TTB recognizes 13
AVAs: Applegate Valley, Columbia Gorge, Columbia
Valley, Dundee Hills, McMinnville, Red Hills Douglas
County, Ribbon Ridge, Rogue Valley, Southern Oregon,
Umpqua Valley, Walla Walla, Willamette Valley
and the Yamhill-Carlton District. There are more
applications pending including Chehalem Mountain
and Eola Hills. It is expected this list will continue
to grow.*

*If an AVA is listed on the label, it is required by law that
at least 85 percent of the grapes used to make the wine
must come from within that AVA.*

Scallops with Wine and Brie

featuring PINOT GRIS

½ lb scallops

salt and freshly ground black
    pepper to taste

2 tsp olive oil

3 cloves garlic, crushed

⅓ cup Pinot Gris

3 oz brie

Scallops are a delicious treat and are generally available year round. When you're shopping look for scallops that are firm and free from any cloudy liquid. If they have a sulfur smell they've spoiled. The world's two most famous scallop shells are probably the one used as the logo for Shell Oil Company and the one featured in Botticelli's masterpiece The Birth of Venus.

1. Preheat the oven to 450°F. If the scallops are exceptionally large you may have to halve or quarter them.

2. Give the scallops a very light sprinkle with salt and pepper, then combine them in a bowl with the olive oil and garlic. Divide the scallops evenly between 4 ramekins and pour the wine over the scallops. The wine should only come about halfway up the scallops.

3. Cut the cheese into slivers and place on top of the scallops. Bake for 15 minutes. Serve with some crusty bread to mop up the juice.

SERVES 4

Buffalo Wings with Blue Cheese Dressing

Whether you have friends over to watch the big game or you're entertaining important dinner guests, Buffalo wings are always a hit. They were invented at the Anchor Bar in Buffalo in the mid-1960s. Today the Anchor Bar claims to dish out more than 1,000 pounds of wings each day! The tasty blue cheese dip is also great with fresh vegetables.

3 lb chicken wings

½ tsp salt

1 tsp cayenne pepper

1 tsp paprika

1 tsp garlic powder

1 cup all-purpose flour

½ cup crumbled blue cheese

¾ cup mayonnaise

¼ cup sour cream

¼ cup butter

⅓ cup white wine

½ cup hot sauce (or to taste)

1. Disjoint the chicken wings and discard the tips. Mix together the salt, spices and flour. Place half the mixture in a large resealable plastic bag and add half of the chicken wings. Shake thoroughly to coat the wings in the flour mixture. Put the rest of the flour mixture in a second bag and repeat the process.

2. Place both bags of chicken wings in the refrigerator for 1–2 hours.

3. Make the dressing by combining the blue cheese, mayonnaise and sour cream in a small bowl. Mix well, cover and refrigerate until you're ready to serve.

4. Preheat the oven to 400°F. Shake the wings in the flour mixture again to ensure they're well coated with flour. Lightly grease two baking trays and arrange the wings on the trays. Cook for 45 minutes, flipping midway through the cooking process.

5. Just before the wings are ready, heat the butter, wine and hot sauce in a small saucepan. Stir until the butter melts. Simmer for 5 minutes. Taste and add more hot sauce if necessary.

6. Place the cooked wings in a large container and immediately cover with the hot sauce. Stir, coating the wings evenly with the sauce.

7. Serve with the blue cheese dressing.

SERVES 6

Baked Crab and Almond Dip

¼ cup sliced almonds

8 oz cream cheese, softened

¼ cup mayonnaise

¼ cup white wine

¼ cup grated Parmesan cheese

¼ cup finely chopped green
    onions

1 clove garlic, crushed

2 dashes hot red pepper sauce

1 can crabmeat, drained well
    (6 oz)

Even people who don't usually like crab love this dip. The almonds provide a wonderful texture and the "cheesy nuttiness" works very well with white wine.

1. Preheat the oven to 350°F. Toast the almonds in a dry pan over medium heat. Stir frequently, making sure not to burn them. Set aside.

2. Combine all the ingredients except the almonds and crab in a medium-sized bowl and stir well. When the mixture is well combined, stir in the crab. Transfer the mixture to a small baking dish. Sprinkle with toasted almonds and bake uncovered for 20–25 minutes, until it's hot and bubbly.

3. Remove from the oven and stir thoroughly. Let it cool for 5 minutes and stir again before serving. Serve with tortilla chips or crusty French bread.

SERVES 6

Sun-Dried Tomato Crostini

The red wine makes these crostini spectacular. The trick is to get a crust on the bottom of the baguette so when you add the wine it doesn't get soggy, but absorbs some of that wonderful wine flavor.

1. Combine the egg, cream, cheese and garlic in a food processor or blender and blend until it has a thick texture similar to pesto. If the mixture is not thick enough, blend a little longer. Transfer to a small bowl.

2. Pulse the basil in the food processor until finely chopped, then add to the cheese mixture.

3. Remove the pits from the olives. Pulse the olives and sun-dried tomatoes in the food processor until finely chopped. Add to the cheese mixture and mix well.

4. Spread the paste on 1 side of each baguette slice.

5. Melt the butter in a large frying pan over medium heat. If your pan is not big enough to hold all the baguette slices, divide the butter and do 2 batches. As soon as the butter begins to bubble, add the baguette slices with the spread side facing up. Cook until golden brown on the bottom, then reduce the heat to medium-low.

6. Remove the pan from the heat and add the red wine directly to the pan—around the bread, not on top! Return the pan to the heat and cover. Cook for 5 minutes, until the cheese has melted. Serve immediately.

SERVES 4–6

1 egg

2 Tbsp whipping cream

1 cup grated Parmesan cheese

1 small clove garlic

1 cup loosely packed fresh basil leaves

¼ cup kalamata olives (with pits)

¼ cup sun-dried tomatoes

10 slices baguette (½ inch thick)

2 Tbsp butter

¼ cup red wine

Bethel Heights Curried Crab Endives

featuring BETHEL HEIGHTS PINOT GRIS

1 Tbsp Pinot Gris

6 Tbsp mayonnaise

2 tsp curry powder

1 clove garlic, crushed

3 Tbsp fresh herbs (chives, oregano, basil, thyme, etc.)

2 Tbsp fresh lemon juice

¾ lb shredded freshly cooked Dungeness crabmeat

salt and freshly ground black pepper to taste

½–¾ lb Belgian endive (about 30 leaves)

¼ lb cherry tomatoes

These curried crab appetizers, created by winery co-owner Marilyn Webb, make a wonderful party platter. As an alternative to endives, try baby bok choy as the "container" for the crab. This recipe also works very well with sautéed rock shrimp. The lush, fruity Bethel Heights Pinot Gris is divine when paired with seafood of any kind.

1. Whisk the wine, mayonnaise, curry powder, garlic, herbs and lemon juice together in a large bowl. Add the crabmeat, mix well and season with salt and pepper. Chill until ready to serve.

2. Carefully separate and clean the endive leaves.

3. Put about 1 Tbsp of the crab mixture on the white root end of each leaf. Arrange on a serving platter and garnish with cherry tomatoes.

SERVES 8–10 (MAKES ABOUT 30 SMALL APPETIZERS)

BETHEL HEIGHTS

6060 Bethel Heights Road NW, Salem
TEL: (503) 581-2262
FAX: (503) 581-0943
www.bethelheights.com
info@bethelheights.com

WINE SHOP, TOURS AND TASTINGS

Open Jun.-Aug., Tue.-Sun. 11 a.m.-
5 p.m. Open Mar.-May and Sep.-Nov.,
weekends only 11 a.m.-5 p.m. Closed
Dec.-Feb. except by appointment.

GETTING THERE

From Portland take I-5 south to the
Salem Parkway exit. Stay on the
parkway to the center of town until it
becomes Commercial Street. Stay in
the center right lane and turn right to
cross the Marion Street Bridge. Stay
to the right crossing the bridge and
follow signs to Wallace Road/Highway
221. Go 6 miles on Wallace Road, then
turn left at the Lincoln store onto Zena
Road. Go 4 miles, then turn right onto
Bethel Heights Road NW. Look for the
"Noble Mountain" sign at that corner.
Go ¼ mile to Bethel Heights Vineyard
on the right.

WINERY HIGHLIGHTS

This was one of the first vineyards in
the Eola Hills. It was also one of the
first vineyards to be certified "Salmon
Safe" by the Pacific Rivers Council.
All the estate-grown wines have
displayed the LIVE logo (see right)
since the 2000 vintage.

LIVE

You might have seen the distinctive LIVE logo that adorns numerous Oregon wine labels and wondered what it means. LIVE stands for Low Input Viticulture and Enology, and it certifies that the winery maintains sustainable growing practices. Started by Ted Casteel of Bethel Heights Vineyard in 1997, the LIVE, Inc. organization has certification links with the International Organization for Biological Control and Salmon Safe.

Member vineyards and wineries commit to a range of restrictions and practices aimed at reducing the use of hard chemicals and pesticides and establishing biodiversity in the vineyard. Inspectors scrutinize crop management practices and ensure growers are meeting the standards set by the organization. Wineries are also required to submit their wines to a tasting panel to make sure the quality associated with the LIVE logo is maintained.

Not every winery that uses biologically friendly means of producing wine is a member of LIVE, but you can be assured that those displaying the logo meet the high standards that have been set. All wines that display the logo are made solely of grapes from certified vineyards and the wine has been made in accordance with LIVE winemaking practices.

Willamette Valley Vineyards Lamb and Goat Cheese Wontons

featuring WILLAMETTE VALLEY VINEYARDS PINOT NOIR

1 tsp dried basil (or 2 tsp chopped fresh basil)

2 tsp paprika

½ tsp cumin

salt and freshly ground black pepper to taste

1 medium onion, cut into ¼-inch cubes

2 Tbsp extra virgin olive oil

1½ cups Pinot Noir

1 sprig rosemary

1 cup lamb stock (or chicken stock)

3 stalks celery, cut in ¼-inch cubes

4 oz soft goat cheese

3 cloves garlic, minced

¾ lb lamb shoulder, minced

1 package small wonton wraps

½ tsp cornstarch

½ cup cold water

vegetable oil for deep-frying

Forrest Klaffke of Willamette Valley Vineyards has come up with this original and delicious recipe especially for this book. The Willamette Valley Vineyards Pinot Noir is one of the most sought-after wines in the United States. Drinking the rest of the bottle with the meal is a must.

1. Place half the basil, 1 tsp of the paprika, the cumin, salt and pepper in a dry pan over medium-high heat. Cook for a few seconds until the pan just barely starts to smoke. Quickly add half the onion and stir to coat. Stir in the olive oil and cook for about 1–2 minutes or until the onion is just starting to become transparent.

2. Remove the ingredients to a blender, add the remaining basil and quickly blend. Return to the pan and add the Pinot Noir and rosemary sprig. Bring to a boil. Turn the heat down to medium or medium-low and let the sauce simmer until reduced by half. Add the lamb stock and simmer on medium or medium-low until the entire mixture has reduced by half again, to about 1 cup. Remove the rosemary sprig and let the sauce cool slightly.

3. In a bowl mix the remaining 1 tsp paprika, the remaining onion, celery, goat cheese, garlic, lamb, salt and pepper.

4. Place about 1 tsp of the mixture in the center of each wonton wrap. Fold the wontons into a pocket by bringing up the middle of each side to the center. Mix the cornstarch with the cold water and use your fingers or a small brush to lightly dab the edges of the wontons to seal them shut. When they are sealed, deep-fry in hot vegetable oil for about 2 minutes or until golden brown. Serve with the dipping sauce.

SERVES 8 (MAKES ABOUT 40 WONTONS)

WILLAMETTE VALLEY VINEYARDS
8800 Enchanted Way SE, Turner
TEL: 1 (800) 344-9463
www.wvv.com
tastingroom@wvv.com

WINE SHOP, TOURS AND TASTINGS
Open daily 11 a.m.–6 p.m. Taste the
vintage selections for free or pay
$6 for a reserve tasting. (You get
a Riedel glass to keep.) Tours by
appointment.

GETTING THERE
Heading south on I-5, take the
Sunnyside/Turner exit 248 and
continue south past the Forest Glen
RV Park and the Enchanted Forest.
The winery is on your left.

WINERY HIGHLIGHTS
Enjoy majestic views and fine wine
atop Illahee Hill. WVV Pinot Noir
was listed as one of the top 15 wines
in the country by *Wine and Spirits*
magazine.

Deviled Eggs with Shrimp

12 large eggs

½ Tbsp dry white wine

½ cup mayonnaise

1 Tbsp Dijon mustard

2 Tbsp fresh herbs, finely chopped (dill, tarragon, chives, basil, etc.)

2 drops hot pepper sauce (or to taste)

salt and freshly ground black pepper to taste

½ lb small, cooked, peeled shrimp

How did such a heavenly dish get such a devilish name? Different historians have different opinions but most believe that it had something to do with hot spices. The key to good deviled eggs is cooking the eggs over low heat; high heat makes them rubbery.

1. For perfect hard-boiled eggs, put the eggs in a saucepan and cover with cold water. Bring to a rapid boil over high heat. As soon as the water boils, turn off the heat and let the eggs sit in the hot water for 15–20 minutes (depending on the size of the eggs). Place them in ice water and crack the shells. The ice water stops them from getting the greenish ring around the outside of the yolk.

2. Carefully peel the eggs and cut them in half lengthwise. Place the yolks in a bowl and mash until smooth with a fork. Add the wine, mayonnaise, Dijon mustard, half the herbs, hot pepper sauce, salt and pepper. Stir thoroughly to blend together. Add the shrimp and gently stir until well combined.

3. Fill the hollow of the egg whites with the shrimp mixture. Sprinkle with the remaining herbs. Cover and refrigerate until you're ready to serve.

SERVES 10–12

Baked Artichokes

The artichoke is probably the world's sexiest vegetable. When selecting an artichoke look for one that's dark green and heavy, with tightly closed leaves. If the leaves are open or a brownish color it's a sign the artichoke is old and will be tougher.

4 whole artichokes

1 lemon, quartered

3 Tbsp olive oil

4 cloves garlic, chopped

salt and freshly ground black pepper to taste

½ cup white wine

½ cup vegetable stock

1. Preheat the oven to 350°F. Place the artichokes under cold running water to wash out any grit from between the leaves. Cut the stems from the artichokes and remove the bottom few layers of leaves as they are too tough to eat. Cut off any thorny tips. Pull back the leaves to expose the inedible center part of the artichoke. Scoop out the "choke" and the purple leaves. A grapefruit spoon works great for this.

2. Using a lemon quarter for each artichoke, rub the lemon any place the artichoke has been cut.

3. Combine the oil, garlic, salt and pepper in a bowl. Place the artichokes in a baking dish and cover with the oil mixture, stuffing some between the leaves.

4. Pour the wine and stock into the bottom of the dish. Cover tightly with foil. Bake for 1 hour.

5. To eat, pull off the leaves and scrape the tender meat from the base of the leaves with your teeth. Some people like to dip the leaves in a mixture of melted butter and lemon juice. We like them plain with a little salt and pepper. The heart is the best part!

Serves 4

Salads

The discovery of a wine is of a greater
moment than the discovery of a constellation.
The universe is too full of stars.

—Benjamin Franklin

Spindrift Cellars Caesar Salad

featuring SPINDRIFT CELLARS WILLAMETTE VALLEY PINOT GRIS

7 anchovy fillets

⅓ tsp freshly ground black pepper

2 cloves garlic

¾ cup extra virgin olive oil

½ cup grated Parmesan cheese

4 large slices Italian or French bread

3 Tbsp Pinot Gris

1 Tbsp fresh fresh lemon juice

1½ tsp dried mustard

1 tsp lemon zest

½ tsp Worcestershire sauce

1 egg

1 large head romaine lettuce

The grapes for this Pinot Gris are grown in the Central Willamette Valley and picked at optimal ripeness. The fruit is whole cluster—pressed and fermented at a cool temperature in stainless steel tanks. A small amount is stored in older French oak barrels to build mouth-feel and complexity when the wine is blended. The result is a brilliant, crisp, food wine with bright flavors of citrus, melon and honey. The lemon in the salad complements the crisp citrus flavors of the Pinot Gris.

1. Preheat the oven to 375°F. Combine the anchovies, pepper, garlic and olive oil in a blender or food processor and process until smooth. Add the Parmesan and blend for another 30 seconds. Set aside ¼ cup of the mixture for the dressing.

2. Brush the remaining mixture evenly over the bread slices and bake for 15–20 minutes in the oven. Remove when bronzed and cut into crouton-sized pieces.

3. Place the remaining dressing mixture in a large glass bowl and add the Pinot Gris, lemon juice, mustard, lemon zest, Worcestershire sauce and egg. Whisk thoroughly and refrigerate until you're ready to serve.

4. Chop the romaine in large pieces and combine with the croutons and dressing. Toss until everything is well coated with dressing.

5. Serve with chilled Spindrift Cellars Pinot Gris.

    SERVES 6

SPINDRIFT CELLARS

810 Applegate Street, Philomath
TEL: (541) 929-6555
FAX: (541) 929-6556
www.spindriftcellars.com
info@spindriftcellars.com

WINE SHOP, TOURS AND TASTINGS
Open weekends 1 p.m.–5 p.m. There
are no tasting fees.

GETTING THERE
From Highway 34/20 turn left on
Eighth Street. It is just one block off
the highway on the corner of Eighth
and Applegate.

WINERY HIGHLIGHTS
With more than 4,000 square feet of
space, the winery is a great place to
host an event or function.

Greek Salad

featuring GAMAY NOIR

1 clove garlic, crushed

½ tsp salt

2 Tbsp Gamay Noir

1 Tbsp fresh lemon juice

1 tsp dried oregano

¼ cup olive oil

1 cucumber, cut in bite-sized
    pieces

2 tomatoes, cut in bite-sized
    pieces

1 green pepper, sliced in
    bite-sized pieces

1 red onion, thinly sliced

1 cup kalamata olives

1 cup crumbled feta cheese

One of the world's oldest cookbooks was written by a Greek, Archestratos, in 330 BC. If this recipe wasn't in there, it should have been. Typical of Greek salads, there is no lettuce in this dish. It's best served at room temperature.

1. Mash the garlic and salt together in a small bowl using the back of a spoon. Add the wine, lemon juice and oregano. Slowly add the oil while whisking vigorously until the mixture is well combined and thickened. (Or place all the dressing ingredients in a jar or sealed container and shake vigorously.)

2. Combine the cucumber, tomatoes, green pepper, onion and olives in a large bowl. Pour the dressing over the top and mix gently. Let the salad marinate for about 30 minutes. Top with the feta cheese just before serving.

SERVES 4

Gamay Noir

pronounced (GA-MAY NA-WHAR)

It was 1395 when Phillip the Bold, Duke of Normandy, ordered all of the Gamay Noir vines to be ripped out of the ground in Burgundy. He even introduced a law saying the variety would never be allowed to grow in Burgundy again. His reasoning was that Pinot Noir would be brought in to replace the outgoing vines.

Fortunately, the grape found a new home in nearby Beaujolais. This variety made its debut in Oregon in the late 1970s when samples from Europe were delivered to Oregon State University. It does well throughout the state and some exceptional wines are produced in the Illinois Valley.

The Gamay Noir grape (the name is sometimes shortened to Gamay) is one of the first to bud and flower, which makes it a potential victim for spring frosts. It usually ripens around halfway through the season. Like the wines in Beaujolais, Gamay Noir does not take long to go from the vine to the store, which is a great advantage for growers. It is not recognized as a wine to cellar and most feel it is best when young.

Gamay Noir is generally a light-colored red wine that is often very fragrant. The wines can be tangy and full of fruit. Gamay Noir can be served slightly chilled and it makes a great accompaniment to red meats, tomato dishes, barbecued food or cheese and crackers.

Troon's Summer Salad

featuring TROON VINEYARD DRUID'S FLUID

1 Tbsp red wine

½ cup raspberry vinaigrette (there are several to choose from)

2–3 cups torn or chopped lettuce

8 strawberries, sliced

⅓ cup candied pecan pieces

¼ cup crumbled blue cheese, (we used Rogue Creamery Oregon Blue Vein)

On a summer's day nothing beats a crisp salad. That is, nothing except a crisp salad and a glass of wine. This recipe was made using Troon's Druid's Fluid, a slightly sweet red blend of Merlot, Syrah, Zinfandel and Cabernet.

1. In a small bowl combine the wine and vinaigrette.

2. Place all the other ingredients in a medium-sized bowl and lightly toss.

3. Add the dressing just before serving. Serve with a glass of Druid's Fluid.

SERVES 2 AS A MAIN OR 4 AS A SIDE DISH

TROON VINEYARDS
1475 Kubli Road, Grants Pass
TEL: (541) 846-9900
FAX: (541) 846-6096
www.troonvineyard.com
info@troonvineyard.com

WINE SHOP, TOURS AND TASTINGS
Open daily for wine tasting 11 a.m.–
6 p.m. Closed during Jan.

GETTING THERE
It's just 20 minutes from either
Jacksonville or Grants Pass. From
Grants Pass take Highway 199 to
Highway 238. Turn left on North
Applegate Road and continue to
Kubli Road. The vineyard is on
the left.

WINERY HIGHLIGHTS
The winery is reminiscent of a
French villa with copper gutters,
tile roof and extensive cedar
work. Inside you'll find hickory
floors, granite countertops and a
commercial kitchen.

Taste of Oregon Salad

featuring MARIONBERRY WINE

¾ cup marionberry wine

1 small shallot, diced

1 Tbsp sugar

¼ cup apple cider vinegar

1 Tbsp Dijon mustard

½ cup canola oil

½ cup hazelnuts, coarsely chopped

12 cups mixed organic greens

½ cup crumbled feta cheese

Marrionberries are an Oregon specialty that the world is just beginning to discover. Each year, between July and August around 30 million pounds of marionberries are picked and eaten fresh or frozen or, more recently, made into marionberry wine. This refreshing salad can be made using other fruit wines; simply adjust the sugar levels to suit your chosen wine. Adding some grilled chicken to this dish turns it into a meal.

1. Mix the wine, shallot and sugar in a small saucepan over medium heat and bring to a boil. Reduce the heat and simmer for 15 minutes.

2. Transfer the mixture to a food processor or blender and add the vinegar and mustard. While blending, slowly add the oil.

3. Place the hazelnuts in a dry pan over medium heat. Stir frequently until lightly toasted, making sure not to burn them.

4. Divide the greens evenly between the plates. Top with desired amount of dressing, hazelnuts and crumbled feta cheese.

SERVES 4

A stunning shot of Willamette Valley Vineyards (page 21) PHOTO COURTESY OF WILLAMETTE VALLEY VINEYARDS

OPPOSITE: Troon's Summer Salad (page 30)

PREVIOUS PAGE: Woolridge Creek Grilled Zucchini and Prosciutto Shrimp (page 12)

Historic Wine Country Farm was built in 1910 and is a B&B as well as a winery (page 47)

OPPOSITE: King Estate Dungeness Crab Strudel (page 60)

Harvest time at King Estate（page 61） RACHELL COE PHOTO

Vineyard manager Daniel Fey with the longhorns at WillaKenzie Estate (page 93) ANDREA JOHNSON PHOTO
NEXT PAGE: Natalie's Estate Grilled Swordfish with Chardonnay and Rosemary Sauce (page 70)

Caprese Salad

During the 1950s, on the Italian island of Capri, Titina Costanzo invented the Caprese salad. She says she created it so local women could "have a nice lunch and still fit into their bikinis." This stunning salad is the red, white and green of the Italian flag. It's very important to use fresh tomatoes and basil. You can use any type of tomatoes as long as they're ripe.

1 small clove garlic, crushed

¼ tsp salt

1 Tbsp white wine

½ Tbsp fresh lemon juice

2 Tbsp extra virgin olive oil

½ lb buffalo mozzarella, sliced

2 large vine-ripened tomatoes, sliced

¼ cup chopped fresh basil

1. Use the back of a spoon to mash the garlic and salt in a small bowl. Add the wine and lemon juice. While whisking rapidly, slowly add the oil.

2. Alternately layer slices of mozzarella, tomato and basil on a serving platter or individual plates. A pinwheel layout is a popular and attractive way to arrange the salad. Drizzle the dressing overtop. Let the salad stand for 5 minutes before serving.

SERVES 4

Soups & Stews

If you have a good wife, good wine and a
rich cabbage soup, look not for other things.

—Russian proverb

August Cellars Maréchal Foch Buffalo Stew

featuring AUGUST CELLARS MARÉCHAL FOCH

1 lb buffalo, cubed

¼ cup all-purpose flour

3 Tbsp olive oil

2 cups roughly chopped carrots

2 cups roughly chopped celery

2 cups roughly chopped onion

¼ cup tomato paste

1½ cups Maréchal Foch

2 cups cubed potatoes

1 Tbsp crushed garlic

1 Tbsp minced ginger

¼ tsp cumin

2 bay leaves

4 cups beef broth

salt and freshly ground black
    pepper to taste

Winery friend Daniel Rich has created this awesome buffalo recipe that highlights the August Cellars Maréchal Foch. This hybrid wine has a big, plummy, slightly earthy flavor. It goes well with game meats, lamb, duck and venison, wild mushrooms, chanterelles, morels and dark chocolate. It is comparable to an old-vine Zinfandel, Merlot or Syrah.

1. Preheat the oven to 325°F. Dredge the buffalo in the flour and shake off any excess. Heat the oil in a large, ovenproof stewpot over medium-high heat. Sear the buffalo for a few minutes, browning on all sides. Remove the meat from the pan and set aside.

2. Add the carrots, celery and onion to the same pot and cook for 5–6 minutes, until slightly browned. Add the tomato paste and pour in the wine to deglaze. Use a wooden spoon to scrape up any browned bits from the bottom of the pot. Add the buffalo, potatoes, garlic, ginger, cumin, bay leaves and broth to the pot.

3. Cook in the oven, partially covered, for about 2 hours or until the meat is tender. Season with salt and pepper. Enjoy with a glass of August Cellars Maréchal Foch.

SERVES 4

AUGUST CELLARS
14000 NE Quarry Rd, Newberg
TEL: (503) 554-6766
FAX: (503) 554-6866
www.augustcellars.com
sales@augustcellars.com

WINE SHOP, TOURS AND TASTINGS
Open daily May–Sep. 11 a.m.–5 p.m.
Open Oct.–Apr., Fri.–Sun. 11 a.m.–
5 p.m. No tasting fee for August
Cellar wines, but other wines
featured do have a tasting fee.

GETTING THERE
Located east of Newberg, just off
Highway 99W. The blue highway
signs on Highway 99W will help with
locating the turn.

WINERY HIGHLIGHTS
August Cellars is a gravity winery
that produces Pinot Noir, Maréchal
Foch, Chardonnay, Gewürztraminer,
Pinot Gris and Riesling. The motto is
"great wines at a fair price."

Chunky Vegetable Soup

3 Tbsp olive oil

2 eggplants, cut in 1-inch cubes

2 medium zucchini, chopped

2 carrots, chopped

2 potatoes, cut in 1-inch cubes

2 Tbsp butter

2 cloves garlic, crushed

1 large sweet onion, chopped

2 stalks celery, chopped

1 lb mushrooms, chopped

1 cup dry white wine

1 can chopped tomatoes
(15 oz)

8 cups vegetable stock

2 Tbsp Worcestershire sauce

salt and freshly ground black
pepper to taste

2 Tbsp cornstarch

¼ cup water

Parmesan cheese for garnish
(optional)

chopped fresh parsley for
garnish (optional)

After a long, cold winter's day there's nothing like coming home to a big, hot pot of vegetable soup. This soup is a great after-work snack and there's no problem keeping leftovers in the fridge for a few days. Cooking some of the vegetables under the broiler first gives the soup a flavor boost.

1. Mix the oil, eggplant, zucchini, carrots and potatoes in a large bowl. Spread the vegetables out on a baking tray and broil for about 15 minutes, tossing them every 5 minutes or so.

2. Melt the butter in a large soup pot over medium heat. Sauté the garlic, onion, celery and mushrooms for about 8–9 minutes until they become soft.

3. Add the broiled vegetables, wine, tomatoes and their juice, stock, Worcestershire sauce, salt and pepper. Bring to a boil and simmer for 25 minutes. Mix the cornstarch with the water and stir the mixture into the pot. Cook and stir to thicken.

4. Sprinkle with Parmesan and parsley, if using. Serve with crusty bread.

Serves 6

The Simplest Pea and Ham Soup

Leftover ham bone after the holidays? Here's a simple way to avoid any waste and get the most from your meat. This soup has an incredible vibrant color and is a healthy treat after indulging in festive eating.

1. Melt the butter in a pot over medium heat. Add the onion, garlic, parsnip, thyme and peas. Sauté for 5 minutes. Add the wine, ham bone and stock and bring to a boil.

2. Reduce the heat and simmer uncovered for 50 minutes. Remove the ham bone.

3. Transfer the soup to a blender or food processor and blend until smooth. Return to the pot to reheat and season with salt and pepper.

4. Great served with a thick slice of buttered bread.

SERVES 4–6

2 Tbsp butter

2 cups chopped onion

2 cloves garlic, crushed

1 parsnip, chopped

2 Tbsp fresh thyme leaves

4-5 cups frozen peas, thawed

1 cup dry white wine

1 ham bone

5 cups stock (pork or chicken)

salt and freshly ground black pepper to taste

Iris Hill's Friday Harbor Fish Soup

featuring IRIS HILL PINOT GRIS

2 Tbsp olive oil

1 onion, chopped

1 green bell pepper, chopped

4 cloves garlic, minced

16 oz clam juice

⅔ cup Pinot Gris

4½ cups chicken stock

1 tsp each dried basil, oregano, thyme

chopped seasonal vegetables (optional, but potatoes are great)

1½ lb cubed fish (snapper and ling cod work well)

½ lb scallops (chop if large)

⅔ cup mayonnaise

¾ tsp cayenne pepper

1 Tbsp wine vinegar

¼ tsp salt

salt and freshly ground black pepper to taste

This fabulous fish soup is easy to make and the spicy mayonnaise gives it a lift. It features the Iris Hill Pinot Gris, a dry wine with a great fruit-to-acid balance that has flavors of tropical fruit, minerals, peach and melon. All fruit comes from the estate vineyard and the wine is fermented and aged in stainless steel.

1. Heat the olive oil in a large pot over medium-high heat. Add the onion, green pepper and half the garlic and sauté 4–5 minutes or until softened. Add the clam juice, wine, chicken stock, basil, oregano, thyme and vegetables (if using). Simmer for 15–30 minutes, until the vegetables are soft.

2. Turn off the heat. Add the fish and scallops, cover and allow to stand. The fish and scallops will cook in the hot soup.

3. Combine the remaining garlic, mayonnaise, cayenne, wine vinegar and ¼ tsp salt in a small bowl.

4. When the fish and scallops are cooked through you can season with salt and pepper. Serve the soup with a dollop of mayonnaise on the side and some crusty bread. Enjoy with a glass of Iris Hill Pinot Gris.

SERVES 4–6

IRIS HILL WINERY
82110 Territorial Road, Eugene
TEL: (541) 895-9877
FAX: (541) 895-9879
www.iris-hill.com
info@iris-hill.com

WINE SHOP, TOURS AND TASTINGS
Open Memorial Day weekend–
Thanksgiving weekend, Thu.–Sun.
noon–5 p.m.

GETTING THERE
The tasting room is located 18 miles
southwest of Eugene near the town
of Lorane.

WINERY HIGHLIGHTS
There are beautiful views to the
southwest overlooking the vineyard.

Mystic's Gazpacho Barbera

featuring MYSTIC BARBERA

1 red bell pepper, chopped

2 Anaheim peppers, seeded and chopped

½ red chili pepper, seeded and chopped

8 cloves garlic

2 English cucumbers, peeled, seeded and chopped

1 medium onion, chopped

12 Roma tomatoes, peeled and seeded

2 Tbsp chopped fresh oregano leaves

1 Tbsp fresh thyme leaves

1 tsp minced fresh rosemary

3½ cups tomato juice

2½ cups Barbera

salt and freshly ground black pepper to taste

Chef Tyna Mays-Shey developed this gazpacho featuring the Mystic Barbera. The soup is best prepared a day ahead to give the flavors time to infuse. The wines produced by Mystic are all reds from small vineyards that are at least 12 years old. Focusing on the individual vineyards, the resulting wines are fruit forward and great with food.

1. This recipe is best done in batches. Place each batch in a non-reactive container once it has been processed.

2. Place all the peppers in a food processor and process until smooth. Add the garlic, cucumbers and onion and process until finely chopped. Remove to the container. Process the tomatoes and herbs, scraping down the bowl as necessary. Add to the soup container.

3. Stir the tomato juice and wine into the mixture. Cover and chill overnight. Season with salt and pepper. Serve chilled.

SERVES 4

MYSTIC WINES

3995 Deepwood Lane NW, Salem

TEL: (503) 581-2769

FAX: (503) 581-2894

www.mysticwine.com

info@mysticwine.com

WINE SHOP, TOURS AND TASTINGS

Open Apr.–Nov., weekends only, noon–5 p.m. Tasting is free.

GETTING THERE

Located about 1 mile north of Hopewell, the winery is just off the Lafayette Highway between Salem and McMinnville.

WINERY HIGHLIGHTS

Since opening in 1992, Mystic has focused on the "Noble Northwest Reds" and the production of small, vineyard-specific lots.

Barbera

pronounced (BAR- BEH-RUH)

This classic red Italian grape variety is still commonly grown in northern Italy, where records show it has thrived since at least 1700. It is believed to have made its way to America some time in the late 1800s. In the United States it has traditionally been used as a blending wine in Californian "jug wines."

Now winemakers have started to focus on Barbera as a wine in its own right and the results have ranged from average to absolutely spectacular. In Oregon, the variety grows well, but it's risky, as production can easily be ruined by fall rain or a nasty spring frost.

There is not much Barbera planted in Oregon and it usually sells out very quickly. It's certainly a variety to try if you manage to get your hands on a bottle.

Barbera is usually made into a full-bodied wine and common characteristics include flavors of blackberry, currants, spices and chocolate, with aromas of smoke, vanilla and cherries. The wine ages well and is great paired with beef, game birds, lamb, pork and hard cheeses.

R. Stuart & Co. Magnificent Duck Stew with Olives

featuring BIG FIRE PINOT NOIR

3 Tbsp olive oil

2 Tbsp butter

3 tsp herbes de Provence

1 lb fresh chanterelles

3 lb boneless skinless duck breasts

1 medium onion, finely chopped

3 cloves garlic, minced

½ cup dry Madeira

¾ cup Pinot Noir

1 lb plum tomatoes, peeled, seeded and chopped (or 1 can peeled tomatoes, 28 oz, drained and chopped

2½ cups mushroom stock

1 bay leaf

1½ cups pitted green olives

2 tsp cornstarch

1 Tbsp sherry wine vinegar

salt and freshly ground black pepper to taste

1½ Tbsp chopped fresh parsley

This recipe should be prepared the day before serving. It truly is magnificent and the preparation is well worth it. The Big Fire label is a whimsical reflection of the winery crew's passion for what they do. Big Fire is blended to be friendly, lively and utterly drinkable. Everyday? Absolutely. Ordinary? Never.

1. Heat 1 Tbsp of the olive oil and the butter in a large flameproof casserole over medium-high heat. Add 2 tsp of the herbes de Provence and the chanterelles and sauté for 5 minutes or until they're browned. Remove from the casserole and set aside.

2. Season the duck liberally with salt and pepper. Heat the remaining 2 Tbsp olive oil and add the duck in 2 batches. Lightly brown on both sides, about 5 minutes per batch. Remove to a plate.

3. Add the onion to the casserole, stirring until softened, about 3 minutes. Add the garlic and cook 1 minute longer. Pour in the Madeira and Pinot Noir. Bring to a boil, scraping the brown bits from the bottom of the pan. Boil until the liquid has reduced by half, 2–3 minutes.

4. Stir the tomatoes into the casserole. Return the duck to the pan along with any juices collected on the plate. Add the stock, remaining 1 tsp of herbes de Provence and the bay leaf. Cover, reduce the heat to low and simmer for 25 minutes.

5. Bring a medium saucepan of water to a simmer. Add the olives and simmer for 25 minutes. Drain the olives in a colander. Add the olives and the sautéed chanterelles to the casserole. Continue to simmer, partially covered, until the duck is tender, 20–30 minutes longer.

R. STUART & CO.
845 NE 5th Street, McMinnville
TEL: (503) 472-6990
FAX: (503) 472-7940
www.rstuartandco.com
maria@rstuartandco.com

WINE SHOP, TOURS AND TASTINGS
Tasting room open May–Oct.,
Mon.–Sat. 11 a.m.–5 p.m. and
Nov.–Apr., Mon.–Fri. 11 a.m.–5 p.m.
All other times by appointment.
There is no charge to taste.

GETTING THERE
Located in downtown McMinnville
just blocks from historic Third Street.

WINERY HIGHLIGHTS
R. Stuart & Co. staked its claim
in downtown McMinnville by
taking over an old granary in
the neighborhood known as the
"Pinot Quarter."

6. Remove the duck breasts and cut them into bite-sized pieces. Skim off any fat from the liquid in the pan. Remove and discard the bay leaf. Boil over high heat to reduce slightly, about 3 minutes. Dissolve the cornstarch in 1 Tbsp of water and stir into the sauce. Boil for about 2 minutes, stirring, until thickened and clear. Return the duck to the pot, cool and refrigerate overnight.

7. Gently rewarm the stew over medium to medium-low heat. Stir in the vinegar and season with salt and pepper. Garnish with parsley. This stew is fantastic served over soft polenta and enjoyed with Big Fire Pinot Noir.

SERVES 6–8

Wine Country Farm's Famous Grilled Portobello Bisque

featuring WINE COUNTRY FARM MÜLLER THURGAU

¼ cup balsamic vinegar

2 Tbsp olive oil

1 tsp chopped fresh thyme

2 cloves garlic, crushed

2 portobello mushrooms
(4 inches across), stemmed,
gills removed

2 Tbsp butter

3 cups roughly chopped wild
mushrooms (such as
crimini, chanterelle, oyster,
morel or stemmed shiitake)

¾ cup thinly sliced leeks
(whites only)

3 cups chicken broth

1 cup Müller Thurgau

1 cup whipping cream

freshly ground black pepper
to taste

Chef Lynn McPherson of Wine Country Farm developed this recipe to highlight the wonderful marriage of mushrooms and wine. The Muller Thürgau is a light semi-dry wine with 1.5 percent residual sugar. The bit of spice in the aftertaste complements some of the spicier foods, such as Thai, Chinese and Mexican. It pairs very well with soups, chicken and pork.

1. Preheat the grill to medium-high. Whisk the vinegar, oil, thyme and 1 crushed garlic clove together in a bowl, blending well. Brush the mixture over the portobellos and grill until the mushrooms are tender and juicy, about 12 minutes per side. Cut into ½-inch-thick strips and set aside.

2. Melt the butter over medium heat and sauté the wild mushrooms and remaining garlic for about 5 minutes. Add the leeks and sauté for 5 minutes more. Add the broth, wine and grilled portobellos. Bring to a boil, then reduce the heat and simmer for another 15 minutes.

3. Remove from the heat and whisk in the cream. Just before serving top with freshly ground black pepper. Serve with a glass of Wine Country Farms Müller Thurgau.

SERVES 8

WINE COUNTRY FARM

6855 Breyman Orchards Road, Dayton

TEL: (503) 864-3446 or

1-800-261-3446

www.winecountryfarm.com

jld@winecountryfarm.com

WINE SHOP, TOURS AND TASTINGS

Open daily between Memorial Day weekend and Thanksgiving weekend, 11 a.m.–5 p.m. During winter the winery is only open weekends. Complimentary tasting available.

GETTING THERE

From Portland take I-5 south toward Salem. Take exit 289 and follow to Highway 99W. Turn left and continue through Newberg and Dundee. Three miles out of Dundee turn right onto McDougall Road. After 1 long block turn right onto Breyman Orchards Road. Wind 2 miles up to the winery.

WINERY HIGHLIGHTS

Wine Country Farm's B&B is the only Willamette Valley wine region B&B included in the *New York Times* #1 bestseller *1000 Places to See Before You Die.*

Müller Thurgau

In 1882, at the famous Geisenheim Institute in Germany, a new variety of grape was developed. The creator was Dr. Herman Müller, who came from the Swiss canton of Thurgau. Only after Dr. Müller died was the grape named after him.

Dr. Müller recorded the new grape's parents as Riesling and Sylvaner, but subsequent DNA testing has led some scientists to conclude that it's impossible for Sylvaner to be a parent and that it's more likely to be Chasselas. The grape's parentage remains a mystery, adding intrigue to the varietal.

The popularity of the grape soared and by the 1970s the variety was Germany's most-planted wine grape. Its glory was short-lived, but although its popularity has declined there are still significant plantings in Germany today.

In the United States the majority of Müller Thurgau plantings are in Oregon. The cooler climate often results in a "summer sipping" wine with just enough acidity.

Müller Thurgau is generally produced as an off-dry wine. Common flavors are pineapple, melons and peaches with aromas of ripe tropical fruits. It is at its best when consumed young. The wine pairs well with a wide range of foods, including spicy curries, hot peppers, chicken tacos and barbecued seafood.

Domaine Coteau Beef Bourguignon

featuring DOMAINE COTEAU PINOT NOIR

6 Tbsp olive oil

3 lb boneless beef chuck, cut into 2-inch pieces

16–20 small white onions, peeled (or 1 package pearl onions)

1 carrot, grated

6–7 shallots, finely chopped

4–5 Tbsp all-purpose flour

2 cups beef stock (homemade is best)

2 cups Pinot Noir

1 Tbsp tomato paste

1 tsp dried thyme

1 herb bouquet (6 sprigs parsley, 2 celery tops, 1 large bay leaf, all tied together)

1 tsp finely chopped garlic

salt and freshly ground black pepper to taste

¾ lb mushrooms, coarsely chopped

Americans have really taken to this French stew made with Pinot Noir. For the best results try and buy your beef chuck in one piece. Pinot Noir from the Domaine Coteau vineyards has great balance and complexity. It is a dark burgundy with a complex bouquet after several years of bottle aging. On the palate the wine has dark fruit flavors. The finish is long, with soft tannins.

1. Preheat the oven to 350°F. Heat 3 Tbsp of the oil in a large heavy frying pan over medium-high heat. Brown the beef in batches of about 6 pieces at a time, then set aside. When the beef is all browned, add the onions and brown for 4–5 minutes. Remove to a baking dish and place in the oven for 40 minutes.

2. While the onions are baking add the carrot, shallots and 1 Tbsp of the oil to the pan. Cook over low heat for 5–7 minutes. Add the flour and stir to form a roux. Cook, stirring constantly, for 15–20 minutes until the roux turns light brown. Do not let it burn. Add the beef stock and Pinot Noir, stirring constantly, and bring to a boil. Add the tomato paste and stir until the sauce thickens and becomes smooth.

3. Remove the onions from the oven and set aside. Reduce the oven temperature to 325°F. Place the browned beef in a casserole and pour the sauce over the beef. Add the thyme, herb bouquet, garlic, salt and pepper. Cover the casserole and place in the oven for 2–3 hours until the beef is tender. The cooking time will depend on the quality of the meat.

DOMAINE COTEAU
258 North Kutch Street, Carlton
TEL: (503) 697-7319
FAX: (503) 636-4652
www.domainecoteau.com
dean.sandifer@comcast.net

WINE SHOP, TOURS AND TASTINGS
Tasting room open Mar.–Nov.,
weekends noon–5 p.m. Tasting fee
is $5 and is refundable with any
purchase.

GETTING THERE
From Portland take 99W south to
Newburg. Take Highway 240 west to
Carlton. If coming from McMinnville
take 99W north to Highway 47 and
follow to Carlton.

WINERY HIGHLIGHTS
The winery has won numerous
medals at major international wine
competitions.

WINERY SPECIAL OFFER
If you show a copy of this book, the
tasting fee will be waived.

4. Heat the remaining 2 Tbsp of oil in a separate pan over
high heat and sauté the mushrooms for 4–5 minutes.
Set aside and cover. When the beef is cooked add the
onions and mushrooms to the stew and return the
casserole to the oven for 15 minutes.

5. Serve the stew directly from the casserole.
Boiled potatoes, buttered noodles or brown rice
and a steamed green vegetable are excellent
accompaniments. Warm crusty bread is a must to mop
up the sauce. Enjoy with a bottle of Domaine Coteau
Pinot Noir.

SERVES 6–8

Fish & Seafood

If white wine goes with fish,
do white grapes go with sushi?

—*Steven Wright*

Aramenta Hazelnut-Crusted Halibut with Beurre Rouge

featuring ARAMENTA CELLAR PINOT NOIR

1 cup hazelnuts, chopped

4 halibut fillets (4 oz each)

2 eggs

4 Tbsp all-purpose flour

1 Tbsp canola oil

1 cup Pinot Noir

¼ cup whipping cream

4 oz cold butter, cubed

salt and freshly ground black pepper to taste

Chef Brad Howard of Willamette Valley Catering came up with this recipe using the delightful Aramenta Pinot Noir. The soil where this Pinot Noir is grown was originally under a hazelnut orchard. The soil influences the flavor of the grapes, and the Pinot Noir has a buttery and nutty finish that works extremely well with the butter sauce and hazelnut crust in this recipe.

1. Toast the hazelnuts in a dry pan over medium heat for 2–3 minutes, until they're toasty and aromatic. Be careful not to burn them. Set aside on a plate.

2. Pat the fillets dry with a paper towel. Beat the eggs with 1 Tbsp of water until well combined and set aside in a shallow bowl. Place the flour on a separate plate. Dip each halibut fillet on 1 side only in flour, then egg, then hazelnuts.

3. Preheat the oven to 350°F. Heat the oil in a frying pan over medium-high heat. Sear each fillet, crust side down, for 2–3 minutes or until browned. Place the fish, crust side up, on a baking pan.

4. Prepare the beurre rouge by reducing the Pinot Noir in a small saucepan over medium or medium-high heat until it becomes syrupy, 10–20 minutes. When it is syrupy, reduce the heat to low and add the cream. Stir in the butter 1–2 pieces at a time, stirring over low heat until well combined. Keep the sauce warm on a very low heat.

5. Bake the crusted halibut for approximately 6–8 minutes or until cooked through. Season with salt and pepper. Serve crusted side up, surrounded by beurre rouge sauce.

SERVES 4

ARAMENTA CELLARS
17979 NE Lewis Rogers Lane,
Newburg
TEL: (503) 538-7230
FAX: (503) 554-8266
www.aramentacellars.com
eddarloon@cs.com

WINE SHOP, TOURS AND TASTINGS
Tasting daily 10:30 a.m.–5 p.m.
Tasting fee of $5 is refundable with
your wine purchase. Large groups
please call ahead.

GETTING THERE
From Newburg head west on
Highway 240 for 4 miles. Turn
right on Dopp Road, then left on
North Valley Road. Turn right on
Lewis Rogers and continue 1 mile to
Aramenta Cellars.

WINERY HIGHLIGHTS
This is currently the only winery in
the Ribbon Ridge AVA that's open
daily. It's small and rustic, with a
beautiful view of the vineyard and
pond. There's also a patio and gazebo
area for guests to enjoy.

Tender Tuna Steaks in Merlot Butter

featuring MERLOT

5 Tbsp butter, cubed

1 onion, finely chopped

2 cloves garlic, crushed

1 cup Merlot

4 tuna steaks (6 oz each)

salt and freshly ground black
    pepper to taste

2 Tbsp olive oil

2 Tbsp fresh tarragon, finely
    chopped

Merlot and tuna are a great pairing—another example that disproves the "white wine with fish" rule. Fresh tuna is a delicacy and Oregon is the place to get it; every year around 20 million tuna pass by the coast. One of the best places in Oregon to fish for tuna is on a charter boat out of Newport.

1. Heat 1 Tbsp of the butter in a small sauté pan over medium heat. Add the onion and garlic and sauté for 2–3 minutes. Add the wine and increase the heat to high, allowing the wine to reduce by about half.

2. Meanwhile, season the tuna steaks lightly with salt and pepper. Heat the oil in a separate sauté pan over high heat. Sauté the steaks for 2 minutes, flip and cook an additional 1–2 minutes for rare or 3–4 minutes for well done. Transfer to a serving plate.

3. When the wine has reduced by half remove the pan from the heat and whisk in the remaining 4 Tbsp of butter and the tarragon. Top the tuna steaks with the Merlot butter and enjoy with a glass of fine Oregon Merlot.

SERVES 4

Pacific Northwest Seafood Cannelloni

Serve this for dinner if you want to make a great impression on someone. It's rich, cheesy and stuffed full of wonderful fresh seafood. Of course, you can adapt the recipe to use whatever seafood you have available.

1. Preheat the oven to 350°F. Bring the stock and wine to a boil in a large saucepan. Add the prawns, scallops and fish and reduce the heat to a simmer. Allow to simmer for 3 minutes. Remove from the heat and strain, reserving the liquid.

2. In a large frying pan heat ¼ cup of the butter over medium heat. Add the onion and cook until it's soft, 2–3 minutes. Add the mushrooms and cook until they become tender, about 5 minutes. Add the tomatoes, basil and ¼ cup of the stock mixture. Bring to a boil and then simmer until the sauce begins to thicken. Add the seafood and stir in the cream. Season with salt and pepper and remove from the heat.

3. To make the sauce, melt the remaining ¼ cup of butter in a saucepan over medium heat. Add the flour and stir for about 1–2 minutes to form a roux. Remove from the heat and slowly add the milk, stirring well all the time. Return to the heat and bring to a boil, then reduce to a simmer, stirring continuously until the sauce thickens. Remove from the heat.

4. Stuff the seafood mixture into the cannelloni tubes and place the tubes in a greased ovenproof dish. Pour the sauce overtop and sprinkle with the cheeses. Bake for 40 minutes or until the cannelloni tubes are soft and tender. Serve with white wine and a crisp green salad.

SERVES 6

2 cups stock (vegetable, fish or chicken)

1 cup white wine

1 lb raw prawns, peeled and chopped

10 oz scallops, diced

1 lb skinless boneless halibut, diced

½ cup butter

1 onion, finely chopped

2 cups finely chopped mushrooms

1 can chopped tomatoes (14 oz)

3 Tbsp chopped basil

2 Tbsp whipping cream

2 Tbsp all-purpose flour

3 cups milk

salt and freshly ground black pepper to taste

16 cannelloni tubes (use the type that doesn't have to be precooked)

4 oz cheddar cheese, grated

4 oz mozzarella cheese, grated

Smoked Salmon Omelet

featuring SAUVIGNON BLANC

5 eggs

1 Tbsp milk

salt and freshly ground black
    pepper to taste

½ cup Sauvignon Blanc

½ cup stock (vegetable, fish or
    chicken)

½ cup whipping cream

½ bunch watercress, finely
    chopped

6 oz smoked salmon

This elegant omelet is bathed in a magnificent watercress and wine sauce. Don't be intimidated by watercress—it's very easy to use and it gives a stylish touch to any meal. Omelets make a great brunch, but this can be served as a starter, lunch or even dinner.

1. Whisk the eggs and milk together in a small bowl. Season with salt and pepper and set aside.

2. Place the wine in a saucepan and cook over medium-high heat until it reduces by half, about 7 minutes. Add the stock and reduce the mixture by half, another 5–6 minutes. Stir in the cream and watercress, bring to a simmer and cook for about 7–10 minutes, stirring occasionally. Remove from the heat, strain and keep warm.

3. Spray a frying pan with cooking spray. (This works better than butter in this recipe as it provides an even greasing that doesn't burn.) Warm the frying pan over medium heat and then add half the egg mixture. Swish the eggs around in the pan so they start to harden on the bottom of the pan. Cook the mixture for 3–4 minutes until the egg is about 75 percent solid and then place half the smoked salmon on half of the pan. By now the edges of the omelet should be getting crispy and be starting to curl away from the pan.

4. Use a spatula to run around the edge of the omelet and then gently fold the omelet in half. (Use your fingers if you want.) Let the folded omelet sit for another minute before removing it from the pan to a warm plate. Repeat the process with the remaining egg and salmon. Serve topped with watercress sauce.

SERVES 2

Sauvignon Blanc

pronounced (SO-VIN-YAWN-BLAHN)

Wine historians seem to agree that the Loire River Valley area in France is the home of Sauvignon Blanc. The grape is especially important to the Pacific Northwest as it pairs so well with seafood, one of the region's specialties. Sauvignon Blanc is also known in the United States as Fumé Blanc, a successful marketing term coined by Robert Mondavi of California's Mondavi winery.

The variety grows in many unlikely places around the world, including Israel and Texas. Southern Oregon has a reputation for its Sauvignon Blanc and exceptional wines have emerged from this region. However, as winemakers become more familiar with the grape excellent examples are appearing all over the state.

Sauvignon Blanc is known for its herbaceous characteristics and often has grassy aromas. Other flavors include citrus, passion fruit, fig, melon and even banana. Some great food pairings are any type of seafood, chicken, pork, goat cheese and dishes that use red peppers and salads.

Elkhorn Ridge Salmon Pot Pie

featuring ELKHORN RIDGE PINOT NOIR RESERVE 777

1½ lb boneless, skinless
   salmon fillets

2 Tbsp olive oil

1 small fennel bulb, thinly
   sliced

1 large shallot, chopped

1 cup sliced mushrooms

1 Tbsp chopped fresh tarragon

1 tsp salt

½ tsp freshly ground black
   pepper

1 Tbsp cornstarch

1 cup water

1 cup Pinot Noir

1 package puff pastry
   (14-17 oz)

This "Reserve" is a very special bottling made exclusively from the rare Dijon 777 clone of Pinot Noir. Black cherry and blackberry fruit overlaid with chocolate, black peppers and clove notes result in a wine with velvety mouth feel and a long elegant finish. This wine has aged for 14 months in French oak barrels.

1. Preheat the oven to 400°F. Cut the salmon into large chunks. In a large pan heat the oil and sauté the salmon over medium-high heat for 3 minutes. Remove the salmon from the pan and set it aside.

2. In the same pan sauté the fennel, shallot and mushrooms until soft, 5–6 minutes. Add the tarragon, salt and pepper. Combine the cornstarch and water, mix well and add to the pan. Add the wine and return the salmon to the pan. Cook for 2–3 minutes. Remove the pan from the heat.

3. Butter 4–6 individual ramekins (or 1 large one) then fill each ramekin at least ⅔ full with the salmon mixture. Cut the puff pastry into rounds about 2 inches larger than the ramekins. Pinch the puff pastry to the sides of the ramekins to secure the pastry lid.

4. Bake for about 15 minutes or until the crust is a crispy golden brown. Serve with a glass of Elkhorn Ridge Pinot Noir 777.

SERVES 4–6

ELKHORN RIDGE VINEYARDS AND WINERY

10895 Brateng Road, Monmouth
TEL: (208) 622-5305
FAX: (208) 622-8334
www.elkhornridgevineyards.com
alfoss@earthlink.net

WINE SHOP, TOURS AND TASTINGS
Call ahead for info on tours and
tastings.

GETTING THERE
From Monmouth head south on
Highway 99; after 1 mile make a right
onto Parker Road. Turn left on Helmick
Road, proceed to Elkins Road and
turn left. When Elkins curves, stay
right and proceed to Brateng Road;
turn right and go to the top of the hill.
When you see the green water tank
on your left you have arrived.

WINERY HIGHLIGHTS
This winery specializes in Pinot Noir
from the finest clones, including
Pommard and Dijon clones 113, 114,
1154 and 777. Ask them about the
difference between the clones.

King Estate Dungeness Crab Strudel

featuring KING ESTATE DOMAINE PINOT GRIS

1¼ lb cooked Dungeness
  crabmeat

3 Tbsp butter

½ cup finely sliced green onion

¼ cup diced celery

1 Tbsp chopped fresh dill

2 tsp finely grated lemon zest

2 Tbsp fresh lemon juice

2 Tbsp high-quality
  mayonnaise

salt and freshly ground black
  pepper to taste

4 sheets filo pastry

½ cup melted butter

1½ Tbsp white wine vinegar

1½ Tbsp Pinot Gris

2 tsp finely minced shallots

4 oz chilled unsalted butter,
  cut into 8 pieces

salt and white pepper to taste

Winery chef DeeAnn Hall used organically certified, estate-grown Pinot Gris to create this recipe. The wine has aromas of honeysuckle, pineapple, pear and peach and flavors of tropical fruits, honey and spice.

1. Preheat the oven to 375°F. Handling the crabmeat gently, place it in a medium-sized mixing bowl. Heat 2 Tbsp of the butter in a pan over medium heat and sauté the green onion and celery for 5 minutes or until soft. Add this to the crab and then add the dill, lemon zest, lemon juice and mayonnaise. Toss lightly with a fork until blended but still a little chunky. Season with salt and black pepper.

2. On a dry surface, lay out a sheet of filo and lightly brush with melted butter. Repeat with the remaining filo sheets until all 4 sheets are stacked. Cut the filo once vertically and once horizontally into 4 equal-sized pieces.

3. Divide the crab mixture into 4, placing a portion on each filo stack. Roll each into a tight cylinder, with the ends tucked in. Brush with melted butter and bake until light brown and crisp, 12–15 minutes.

KING ESTATE

80854 Territorial Road, Eugene

TEL: (541) 942-9874

FAX: (541) 942-9867

www.kingestate.com

info@kingestate.com

WINE SHOP, TOURS AND TASTINGS

Visitor center open daily 11 a.m.–
6 p.m. Wine tasting and winery
tours are complimentary. You can
also buy fresh-baked breads and
artisan cheeses.

GETTING THERE

Coming from the north on I-5, head
south past Eugene. Take exit 182 at
Creswell West on Oregon Avenue
(which becomes Camas Swale Road
and then Ham Road) to Territorial
Highway. Turn left on Territorial and
the winery is about 2½ miles down
the road.

WINERY HIGHLIGHTS

Try the food and wine pairings
available Wednesday through to
Saturday.

4. Meanwhile, combine the vinegar, wine, shallots, salt, white pepper and the remaining 1 Tbsp melted butter in a small, non-reactive saucepan. Boil over medium heat until the liquid has reduced to about 1 Tbsp. Remove from the heat and add a few pieces of the chilled butter, whisking until they have melted into the reduction. Return the saucepan to the burner and, over very low heat, add the remaining pieces of butter 1 at a time, whisking constantly. The sauce should be creamy in texture and pale in color. Season with salt, white pepper and/or lemon juice.

5. Keep the sauce in a warm spot until you're ready to serve. Slice each strudel diagonally into 2 halves and serve with the sauce and a glass of King Estate Pinot Gris.

SERVES 4

Baked Shrimp with Feta

featuring RIESLING

1½ Tbsp olive oil

½ cup finely chopped onion

1 crushed clove garlic

½ cup Riesling

4 tomatoes, chopped

1 tsp salt

1 tsp freshly ground black
    pepper

1½ Tbsp butter

1 lb large raw shrimp, peeled
    and deveined

1 Tbsp fresh lemon juice

½ tsp dried oregano

1 Tbsp chopped fresh parsley

¾ cup crumbled feta

This Greek dish is known as "Garides Me Feta" and is very popular in the Greek Islands. It has been included here as a main dish but also makes a great appetizer for 4.

1. Preheat the oven to 375°F. Heat the oil in a large frying pan over medium heat and sauté the onion and garlic for 5 minutes or until soft. Add the wine, tomatoes, salt and pepper and simmer for 12–15 minutes, until the sauce is slightly thickened.

2. In a separate frying pan melt the butter and sauté the shrimp until they're pink, about 3–5 minutes. Take care not to overcook. Sprinkle with lemon juice, add the oregano and parsley, then mix well over the heat.

3. Transfer the shrimp to a casserole dish. Cover with the tomato mixture and stir gently, but thoroughly. Sprinkle with the feta, pressing the cheese lightly into the sauce. Place in the oven for about 15 minutes or until the mixture is bubbling.

4. Serve immediately with a slice of crusty bread and a glass of Riesling.

SERVES 2

Riesling

pronounced (REEZ-LING)

The Riesling grape, also known as Johannesburg Riesling, Rhine Riesling or White Riesling, has its origins in the Rhine and Mosel river valleys in Germany. The grape thrives in cool climates and is very resistant to frosts. Rieslings can differ in style and can be sweet or dry, although a semi-dry wine is probably the most common.

The Von Pessls brothers and their friend Adam Doerner are reported to have produced Riesling in southern Oregon during the 1890s, although prohibition put an end to Oregon's legal winemaking activities in 1919. In 1961, the varietal returned when Richard Sommer planted a field of Riesling for Hillcrest Vineyard, which he opened in 1963. Riesling has become a favorite of many wine drinkers throughout the world and Oregon now produces some of the very best Riesling wines.

Riesling is notoriously late to ripen and is usually the last crop of the year to be harvested, as exhausted growers wait patiently for the grapes to reach the desired sugar levels. Rieslings usually have perfumey aromas and fresh fruit flavors. The wine is well suited to many types of food, from fish and seafood to Mexican and Asian fare. Even sushi and curry can be paired with this versatile wine.

LaVelle Vineyards Riesling Curried Prawns

featuring LaVELLE VINEYARDS ESTATE BOTTLED RIESLING

36-40 medium raw prawns,
  peeled and deveined

¼ tsp salt

¼ tsp freshly ground black
  pepper

2 tsp canola oil

1 Tbsp butter

½ cup diced yellow onion

1 Tbsp diced garlic

2 tsp grated fresh ginger

½ cup Riesling

1 Tbsp yellow curry paste

6 oz coconut milk, well shaken

¼ cup sliced green onion

2 cups prepared steamed rice

Chef John-Patrick Downey-McCarthy of the LaVelle Wine Bar and Bistro created this unique and very simple curried prawn recipe. The vineyard has long been known as a site that consistently produces Riesling grapes of exceptional quality and character. The 2005 LaVelle Estate Bottled Riesling used to create this dish is a semi-sweet, Kabinett-style Riesling with aromas and flavors that hint of peach and apricot. The sweetness of this wine is beautifully balanced with a crisp, refreshing acidity that lingers on the finish. This dish can be a little spicy; to make it less so, use a mild curry paste.

1. Dust both sides of the prawns with salt and pepper. Heat the oil in a large sauté pan over high heat, and when the oil is hot add the prawns. Flip the prawns to sear the other side after 10 seconds. Add the butter and cook for 30 seconds longer.

2. Remove the prawns from the pan and add the onion, garlic and ginger. Sauté until golden brown, 2–3 minutes. Remove the pan from the heat and add the Riesling. Return the pan to the burner, add the curry paste and stir.

3. Cook until the mixture is reduced by half, then add the coconut milk. Continue cooking until reduced by half again. Return the prawns to the pan for 30 seconds along with the green onions.

4. Toss to mix in the pan. Serve over rice.

SERVES 2–4

LAVELLE VINEYARDS

89697 Sheffler Road, Elmira

TEL: (541) 935-9406

FAX: (541) 935-7202

www.lavelle-vineyards.com

lvvineyard@aol.com

WINE SHOP, TOURS AND TASTINGS

Tasting room open daily noon–5 p.m.
Tasting is free. Also visit LaVelle Wine
Bar & Bistro in downtown Eugene's
historic Fifth Street Public Market.
Open Sun. and Mon. noon–6 p.m.,
Tue.–Sat., noon–10 p.m. Complimentary
tasting all day Sun.–Mon. and before
5 p.m. Tue.–Sat.

GETTING THERE

To get to the winery, take Highway
126 west from Eugene to Veneta. Turn
right onto Territorial Road, left onto
Warthen Road, right onto Sheffler
Road, and right into the property.

WINERY HIGHLIGHTS

LaVelle Vineyards was planted
in 1968, and the winery license
obtained in 1972, making it the oldest
in the Southern Willamette Valley.
LaVelle holds many events at the
winery, including bi-monthly murder
mystery dinners, holiday open
houses, summer concerts and parties
for its wine club members.

WINERY SPECIAL OFFER

Show your copy of this book and
receive 10 percent off your purchases
at LaVelle Vineyards.

Halibut with a Dill Sauce

featuring SAUVIGNON BLANC

4 halibut fillets (6–8 oz each)

salt and freshly ground black pepper to taste

2 cups fresh dill, chopped

½ cup fresh lemon juice

1 cup Sauvignon Blanc

¼ cup cold butter, cubed

The world's biggest halibut was caught in Alaska and weighed a whopping 440 pounds! In Oregon they don't get that big, though fish around 70 pounds are fairly common. Some anglers believe the best meat comes from halibut weighing 15 to 30 pounds. This size of fish is known as "chicken of the sea" because of its firm and delicious flesh.

1. Preheat the oven to 350°F. Season the halibut fillets well with salt and pepper. Arrange half the dill on the bottom of a baking pan. Place the fillets on top of the dill and cover with the remaining dill.

2. Mix the lemon juice and wine in a bowl and pour it over the fish. Dot the butter over the fish. Cover and bake for about 20 minutes, then remove the cover and bake for another 5–10 minutes or until the fish is cooked through. Remove the fish to plates and keep warm.

3. Transfer the sauce to a small pan and reduce a little further, 2–5 minutes (depending on how much sauce you have left). Drizzle it over the fish and serve immediately.

SERVES 4

Salmon with Lemon Chive Sauce

*Chives have a mild onion flavor that's great for seafood dishes.
If you grow your own chives, you may also want to use the chive
flowers as an edible garnish. Bear in mind, however, that when
chives flower the flavor of the leaves becomes a lot more intense.*

4 salmon steaks (6 oz each)

salt and freshly ground black
pepper to taste

2 Tbsp olive oil

¼ cup white wine

2 Tbsp fresh lemon juice

¼ cup cold butter, quartered

2 Tbsp finely chopped fresh
chives

8 whole chive leaves for
garnish

1. Preheat the oven to 400°F. Season the salmon steaks with
   salt and pepper. Heat the oil in a large frying pan over high
   heat. Add the steaks and sear for 1½ minutes on each side.
   Place on a preheated tray and bake for 7 minutes or until
   barely cooked through.

2. Combine the wine and lemon juice in a small heavy
   saucepan, bring to a boil and simmer over medium heat
   until the liquid is reduced to about 1 Tbsp. Remove from
   the heat and add the butter piece by piece, whisking
   the whole time until it is completely melted. Stir in the
   chopped chives.

3. Spoon the sauce over the salmon and serve. Place 2 whole
   chives atop each steak to garnish.

SERVES 4

St. Innocent's Steamed Mussels

featuring ST. INNOCENT PINOT BLANC

4 lb live mussels

8 slices baguette, cut diagonally

¼ cup olive oil

1 bulb fennel

2 medium onions, diced

2 large carrots, diced

2 large stalks celery, diced

3 bay leaves

1 tsp dried basil (or 1 small bunch fresh Thai basil, finely chopped)

5 cloves garlic, peeled and halved

½ tsp salt

generous grind of black pepper

1½ cups Pinot Blanc

1 cup water (or chicken stock)

Pinot Blanc matches extremely well with shellfish, especially mussels. About three-quarters of the Pinot Blanc is fermented in a stainless steel tank, the rest in older oak barrels. The tank-fermented wine retains a purity of fruit and the barrel-fermented portion adds a nice mouth feel. Tropical fruit aromas and baked apple and pear flavors enhance the sweetness and the rich flavor of shellfish.

1. Discard any mussels with damaged shells and those that are partially open. Scrub the mussels and remove any beards by tearing them out of the shell.

2. Brush 1 side of the baguette slices with some of the olive oil and toast under a broiler until lightly brown. Set aside to cool.

3. Cut the feathery fronds from the fennel and chop coarsely. Discard the top and outer layer of the bulb. Chop the bulb into ¼-inch strips, discarding the core.

4. Heat the remaining olive oil in a large, heavy-bottomed stockpot over medium-high heat. Sauté the onion for 1–2 minutes, stirring often, until softened. Add the chopped fennel bulb and fronds, carrots, celery, bay leaves, basil, garlic, salt and pepper. Stir frequently until softened and aromatic, 5–10 minutes.

ST. INNOCENT WINERY
1360 Tandem Avenue NE, Salem
TEL: (503) 378-1526
FAX: (503) 378-1041
www.stinnocentwine.com
markv@stinnocentwine.com

WINE SHOP, TOURS AND TASTINGS
Tasting room open weekends noon–
5 p.m. or by appointment.

GETTING THERE
Take I-5 to Salem Parkway. Turn
south onto Cherry Avenue and turn
left at Van Ness, the first left. At the
end of Van Ness turn left onto Del
Webb. Turn right at the first street,
Tandem Avenue. St. Innocent Winery
is on your right.

WINERY HIGHLIGHTS
The winery is open twice a year for
special food and wine-tasting events,
on Memorial Day weekend and
Thanksgiving weekend. Check the
website for details.

5. Place the mussels on top of the vegetables. Add the wine and water quickly and cover immediately in order to trap the steam in the pot. Cook covered for 5–8 minutes, then use tongs to remove the opened mussels to a heated bowl. Cover the pot and cook 3 minutes longer. Remove the opened mussels to the bowl and discard any that have not opened.

6. Ladle about ½ cup of the broth and vegetables into 4 preheated bowls and top with the mussels. Garnish with toasted baguette slices and serve immediately.

SERVES 4

Natalie's Estate Grilled Swordfish with Chardonnay and Rosemary Sauce

featuring NATALIE'S ESTATE ROCK HORSE RANCH CHARDONNAY

4 swordfish steaks (6 oz each, 1–1½ inches thick)

2 Tbsp olive oil

2½ tsp chopped fresh rosemary

salt and freshly ground black pepper to taste

6 Tbsp minced shallots

6 Tbsp Chardonnay

3 Tbsp fresh lemon juice

½ cup chilled butter, cut into 8 pieces

Winery Chef Mike Rooney created this recipe using the Rock Horse Ranch Chardonnay. The wine contains melon and floral aromas with a hint of crisp apple flavors. The wine is unoaked so the true expression of the grape is revealed in this dish.

1. Heat the grill to medium-high. Brush the fish with oil and sprinkle with 2 tsp of the rosemary, salt and pepper.

2. Combine the shallots, wine and lemon juice in a small saucepan. Boil over high heat until the liquid is reduced to 2 Tbsp, about 5 minutes. Remove from the heat, add the remaining ½ tsp of rosemary and a piece of butter, whisking until melted. Place the pan over low heat and add the remaining butter a piece at a time, whisking until each piece melts before adding the next. Remove from the heat and season with a little more salt and pepper.

3. Meanwhile, grill the fish until it's opaque in the center, about 3 minutes per side. Serve with the Chardonnay and rosemary sauce, some potatoes and steamed green vegetables. Grab a glass of Rock Horse Ranch Chardonnay and toast a job well done.

SERVES 4

NATALIE'S ESTATE WINERY

16825 NE Chehalem Drive, Newberg
TEL: (503) 554-9350
www.nataliesestatewinery.com
bteegarden@earthlink.net

WINE SHOP, TOURS AND TASTINGS

Call the owners of the winery to arrange a private tasting. International cheeses and chocolates are available to accompany the wines at the tasting.

GETTING THERE

Take North Valley Road off Highway 219 and head west for about ½ mile. Turn right on Chehalem Drive and continue for almost 1 mile to the winery.

WINERY HIGHLIGHTS

The winery handcrafts small quantities of Cabernet Sauvignon, Merlot, Meritage, Syrah, Viognier, Chardonnay and Pinot Noir. The single vineyard wines have intense varietal character and are reflective of their terroir. The winery also offers catered receptions and dinners.

Chardonnay

pronounced (SHAR-DOE-NAY)

Chardonnay is probably still the world's hippest grape and it's the most popular white variety sold in the United States. Its origins can be traced back to Burgundy's Côte d'Or and this is the grape that wine-makers in France turn into the famous white Burgundy wines. Many believe the artistry of the winemaker is most apparent in Chardonnay, as small mistakes made anywhere in the process are very difficult to remedy.

Chardonnay was recently the most commonly grown white in Oregon, but in the year 2000 it fell behind Pinot Gris. Chardonnay has a long history in Oregon, where the climate is perfect for this variety. There are currently numerous "types" or "clones" of Chardonnay planted in Oregon and in recent years the "Dijon" clones have been receiving a lot of attention and great press. With fabulous wines coming from each of the clones, the only way to make a solid judgment is to get out there and try them.

Chardonnay is often aged in oak barrels, which can give the wine overtones of vanilla or buttery toast. In the 1990s, some wineries started producing unoaked Chardonnay and the trend has really taken off. Try an unoaked version and then an oaked one to discover what effect the oak has on the flavor. Chardonnay can be aged in the bottle, although it will not last as long as most red wines.

Chardonnay is almost always dry. It can contain diverse flavors, from citrus to apples; even figs and pineapple are not uncommon. Wonderful pairings for Chardonnay include fish, mussels, lobster, crab, chicken and pork.

Poultry

I'm drinking wine . . . and eating chicken!
And it's good!

—*Leslie Neilson as Dracula in the Mel Brooks movie*
  Dead and Loving it

Anthony Dell Cellars Chicken with Yam Compote

featuring ANTHONY DELL PINOT GRIS (DEL RIO VINEYARD)

4 chicken breasts with ribs

dry Cajun rub to taste

salt and freshly ground black pepper to taste

3 Tbsp olive oil

1 large yellow onion, chopped

1 small head garlic (or to taste), finely chopped

2 medium yams, cubed

1½ cups Pinot Gris

1 Tbsp cornstarch

1 cup whipping cream

This recipe takes a long time to prepare, but WOW! Though the preparation is lengthy, it's simple and the results will astound your dinner guests. The fruit for this wine came from a great vineyard in the Rogue Valley, southern Oregon. Warm temperatures in late September provided fully ripe fruit. After fermentation the wine was aged 7 months in French oak. On the nose and in the mouth this wine gives tropical fruit flavors of pineapple, mango and peach.

1. Preheat the oven to 250°F. Rub the chicken with the dry Cajun rub, salt and pepper.

2. Heat the oil in a 12-inch cast iron frying pan over medium-high heat and brown the chicken, about 8 minutes. Set the chicken aside, then add the onion, garlic and yams to the pan and sauté for about 8 minutes.

3. Return the chicken to the pan, add the wine, cover and bake for 4 hours. Remove the cover and bake 1 hour more until the skin is brown and crispy.

4. Remove the chicken. Mash the onion, garlic and yam to make a compote. Put the skillet on the stove over medium heat and bring to a boil. Mix the cornstarch with a little water in a glass to make a slurry and stir it into the mixture. Allow to reduce for about 5 minutes if necessary. Reduce the heat to a simmer, add the cream and simmer for about 5 minutes.

5. Spoon the compote on a plate and place the chicken on the compote. Pour some Anthony Dell Pinot Gris in your glasses, toast your luck for not being the chicken and enjoy!

SERVES 4

ANTHONY DELL CELLARS
845 Fifth Street, # 300, McMinnville
(see tasting room address below)
TEL: (503) 910-8874
www.anthonydellcellars.com
info@anthonydellcellars.com

WINE SHOP, TOURS AND TASTINGS
The Anthony Dell tasting room
is located inside Café Noir at 610
Marion Street in Salem. Café Noir
tasting room open Wed.–Sat., noon–
6 p.m. The winery is open Memorial
Day weekend from Sat.–Mon. noon–
5 p.m. and Thanksgiving weekend
Fri.–Sun. noon–5 p.m.

GETTING THERE
Both the winery and tasting room are
easy to find. The tasting room is in
downtown Salem and the winery is in
downtown McMinnville.

WINERY HIGHLIGHTS
Anthony Dell is a micro-winery that
has won numerous gold medals for
their wine. To this they say "BIG
DEAL!" They want you to try the wine
and make up your own mind.

Pinot Gris

pronounced (PEE-NO-GREE)

Pinot Gris is a mutation of the Pinot Noir grape.
It is known as Pinot Grigio in Italy (and parts
of California), Tokay d'Alsace in France and
Grauburgunder or Rülander in Germany. Originally
from Burgundy, it has been around since the Middle
Ages. Gris means "gray" in French, and this refers
to the color of the grapes. In Oregon the grapes are
usually more golden than gray and even pinkish tones
are not unusual.

The Pinot Gris grape first made an appearance in
Oregon in the mid-1960s. It's generally believed that
David Letts of Eyrie Vineyards planted the first cuttings
and produced North America's first Pinot Gris wine.
The once unknown varietal has taken off and Oregon
Pinot Gris is now esteemed throughout the world. The
northern Oregon climate is perfect for the grape and the
natural acidity in the soil produces clean fresh flavors
in the wine. In hotter climates the grape doesn't seem to
do as well.

Pinot Gris can be tangy and light or rich and full
bodied, depending on the ripeness of the grapes and
the techniques used to create the wine. The wine is
full of lively flavors and generally contains aromas of
fresh fruits, such as pear, melon and apple. It pairs
beautifully with fish and seafood and is great with
sushi. It will also hold up against strong cheeses, such
as brie and even Stilton.

Wine and Honey-Roasted Turkey with Gravy

1 cup white wine

¾ cup butter

2 shallots, finely chopped

¼ tsp dried basil

1 bay leaf

4 cups chicken broth

¼ cup honey

1 turkey (12 lb)

2 carrots, halved lengthways

6 cloves garlic

1 onion, unpeeled and quartered

4 Tbsp all-purpose flour

salt and freshly ground black pepper to taste

This is a fantastic way to roast turkey that's simple enough for even a novice cook. It's guaranteed to produce juicy meat and a tasty gravy.

1. Preheat the oven to 350°F. In a saucepan over high heat combine the wine, ½ cup of the butter, shallots, basil, bay leaf and 3 cups of the chicken broth. Bring to a boil, then reduce to a simmer for 15 minutes. Remove from the heat and stir in the honey.

2. Season the turkey well with salt and pepper. Carefully rub the remaining ¼ cup of butter between the skin and the meat and over the breasts, thighs and drumsticks. Tie or skewer the legs together and place in a roasting pan on a wire rack. Drop the carrots, garlic and onion into the bottom of the pan. Baste the turkey all over with the wine mixture and place in the oven. About every 25–30 minutes baste the turkey with the juices from the bottom of the pan. Cook for about 3 hours until a meat thermometer inserted into the thickest part of the thigh reads 180°F. Remove the bird from the oven, cover it loosely with aluminum foil and let it rest while you make the gravy. Allowing the bird to rest for 30 minutes before carving makes it much juicier.

3. Pour the liquid from the roasting pan into a bowl or large glass measuring jug and set it aside. Discard the onion, garlic cloves, carrots and bay leaf. Add the remaining 1 cup of chicken broth to the roasting pan and use a wooden spoon to scrape up all the browned bits from the bottom of the pan. Add this mixture to the drippings. Allow the drippings to sit for a few minutes until the fat rises to the top. Remove the fat and reserve 4 Tbsp of it.

4. Place the reserved fat in a saucepan over medium heat. Whisk the flour into the hot fat. It is important to have equal portions of fat and flour. Stir until the flour takes on a golden color, then slowly start adding the reserved pan drippings while continually whisking. You should add a total of 3–4 cups. Stir until the gravy is simmering and thick. The gravy will continue to thicken when it is removed from the heat.

5. Carve the turkey and serve with the gravy and your favorite vegetables.

SERVES 8—10

Benton-Lane Smoked Chicken Risotto

featuring BENTON-LANE ESTATE PINOT NOIR

2 Tbsp olive oil

1 onion, diced

1 cup arborio rice

2 cups Pinot Noir

1 can diced tomatoes (15 oz)

3 cans chicken broth
   (14–16 oz each)

1 cup diced smoked chicken

1 cup frozen peas

½ cup grated Parmesan cheese

salt and freshly ground black
   pepper to taste

Smoked chicken is available in many grocery and specialty stores, but you can also make your own using the chef's tip on page 79. This dish is fabulous with Pinot Noir. Winery owner Steve Girard likes his Pinots silky and he makes them with a few tricks that bring out the rich cherry flavors.

1. Heat the olive oil over medium-high heat. Add the onion and sauté for about 5 minutes. Add the rice and cook for a further 2 minutes.

2. Add the Pinot Noir and tomatoes with their juice and lower the heat to a high simmer. Let the mixture reduce for about 10 minutes, stirring frequently. Add a little chicken broth and keep stirring. Keep adding a little more broth whenever the liquid begins to dry out around the rice. Don't forget to keep stirring! It should take around 30 minutes and the rice should be quite tender. Add the chicken, peas and Parmesan and continue stirring until the peas are soft and juicy. Season with salt and pepper.

3. Serve in warmed soup bowls with a glass of Benton-Lane Pinot Noir.

SERVES 6

BENTON-LANE WINERY

23924 Territorial Highway, Monroe

TEL: (541) 847-5792

FAX: (541) 847-5791

www.benton-lane.com

info@benton-lane.com

WINE SHOP, TOURS AND TASTINGS
Tasting daily, Labor Day through to
Thanksgiving.

GETTING THERE
The winery is located 1 mile south of
Monroe on the Territorial Highway.

WINERY HIGHLIGHTS
This is a family-owned winery
founded in 1988 by Steve and Carol
Girard. It's one of only a few that
produce their Pinot Noir entirely from
"certified sustainable" estate-grown
grapes. (See the LIVE reference on
page 19.)

CHEF'S TIP

If you don't own a smoker, you can use a charcoal barbecue to smoke the chicken. Build a small charcoal fire on one side. Once it flames, add several pieces of smoke-wood and place a cut-up chicken on the other side of the grill. Open the vents halfway. Check the fire every hour and add more charcoal or wood if necessary. Remove the chicken after 3 hours.

Carabella Grilled Game Hens with Apricot Tarragon Glaze

featuring CARABELLA VINEYARD PINOT NOIR

2 Tbsp olive oil

¼ cup finely minced sweet onions (Hermiston onions if possible)

freshly ground black pepper to taste

½ tsp chopped fresh tarragon

¼ cup apricot preserves

¼ cup Pinot Noir

1 Tbsp Dijon mustard

4 game hens, split in half

This recipe was tested with the Carabella Vineyard 2005 vintage. The wine, a blend of five clones grown at Carabella Vineyard, has depth of color, dark fruit character and supple complexity. The apricot glaze gives a tang to the grilled game hens. Together they're a perfect match for this wine.

1. Heat 1 Tbsp of the oil in a saucepan over medium-high heat and sauté the onion until golden, about 5 minutes. Add a few grinds of black pepper and the tarragon, apricot preserves, wine and mustard and mix well.

2. Cook until the marinade has a thick syrupy consistency, up to 10 minutes. Remove from the heat and set aside.

3. Brush the split game hens lightly with olive oil. Grind more black pepper onto the skin side and rub it in well.

4. Grill the birds over medium heat with the ribs facing down for 5 minutes. Rotate and flip so the skin side is down and grill a further 5 minutes.

5. Flip the skin side up and generously brush on the glaze. Cook until the glaze sets and the birds are cooked through, up to 35 minutes depending on the size of the hens. Serve with a big, fresh salad.

SERVES 4

CARABELLA VINEYARD

At this time Carabella is a vineyard and the wines are made at a local winery. It is not open for visitors.
TEL: (503) 699-1829
www.carabellawine.com
pinot@carabella.com

WINE SHOP, TOURS AND TASTINGS
Wine is poured during the Memorial Day weekend and Thanksgiving weekend tastings. See website for details.

WINERY HIGHLIGHTS
The 49-acre vineyard was planted in the spring of 1996. There are 5 clones of Pinot Noir as well as Chardonnay and Pinot Gris.

Del Rio Vineyards Baked Olive and Artichoke Chicken

featuring DEL RIO PINOT GRIS

4 chicken breasts (bone in and skin on), halved

6 chicken drumsticks

2 jars marinated artichoke hearts (6½ oz each), quartered

1 jar black olives (6 oz), drained and pitted

½ cup Pinot Gris

½ cup chicken broth

1 Tbsp chopped fresh tarragon

salt and freshly ground black pepper to taste

The Pinot Gris finishes the baked chicken nicely in this Mediterranean-inspired dish. The spicy, aromatic wine leads with scents of pear, apple, wildflower honey and Asian spices. The crisp acidity pumps up the fruit flavors.

1. Preheat the oven to 350°F. Place the chicken in a 9- x 13-inch baking dish with the breasts bone side down. Spread the artichokes and olives around the chicken.

2. Mix the wine and broth together in a small bowl and pour the mixture over the chicken.

3. Sprinkle the chicken with tarragon and season well with salt and pepper. Bake for 1 hour or until the chicken is cooked through and the juices run clear.

4. Serve with garlic mashed potatoes and a glass of Del Rio Vineyards Pinot Gris.

SERVES 4–6

DEL RIO VINEYARDS
52 North River Road, Gold Hill
TEL: (541) 855-2062
FAX: (541) 855-1222
www.delriovineyards.com
rob@delriovineyards.com

WINE SHOP, TOURS AND TASTINGS
Tasting room open daily during
winter 11 a.m.–5 p.m. and during
summer 11 a.m.–6 p.m. There is a $5
tasting fee. Winery tours occur every
Sat. throughout the summer.

GETTING THERE
Del Rio Vineyards is ¾ mile from exit
43 off I-5.

WINERY HIGHLIGHTS
With over 200,000 vines producing
a diverse selection of varieties, Del
Rio is a key grape supplier for many
fine winemakers.

EdenVale Syrah Duck

featuring EDENVALE SYRAH

2 whole ducks

1 head garlic, split crosswise

2 cups water

2 large yellow onions, coarsely chopped

2 large carrots, coarsely chopped

4 large stalks celery, coarsely chopped

2 bay leaves

½ Tbsp freshly ground black peppercorns

½ Tbsp ground fennel seeds

1 Tbsp kosher salt

¾ bottle Syrah

2 cloves garlic, minced

1 tsp minced fresh parsley

1 tsp minced fresh thyme

This duck recipe will impress everyone. The first two steps are best done the day before serving. EdenVale Syrah is produced in the Rogue Valley of southern Oregon, with grapes sourced from multiple vineyards across this diverse wine-growing area.

1. Discard the duck livers but reserve the necks, hearts and gizzards to roast with the bones. Remove the breasts by following along either side of the breastbone with a sharp knife; stay as close to the breastbone as possible. Continue to slice down along the ribs until the breast is freed from the carcass. Repeat on the other side, and trim the excess skin from around the breast. Flip the duck over and remove the legs. First pop the hip ball out of its socket, then free the leg from the body with the knife. Cover the breasts and legs and place them in the refrigerator.

2. Preheat the oven to 400°F. Roast the carcasses, necks, hearts, gizzards and the head of garlic in a 2-inch-deep roasting pan until toffee brown, about 30 minutes. Pour off the excess fat and deglaze the pan with the water, scraping the browned bits from the bottom of the pan. Place the bones, onions, carrots, celery, bay leaves and the liquid in a stockpot. Add enough water to barely cover the bones and simmer 4–6 hours. Strain the stock, discarding the solids, and refrigerate overnight.

EDENVALE WINES
2310 Voorhies Road, Medford
TEL: (541) 512-2955
FAX: (541) 512-2957
www.edenvalewines.com
wine@edenvalewines.com

WINE SHOP, TOURS AND TASTINGS
Summer: open Mon.–Sat. 10 a.m.–
6 p.m.; Sun. noon–4 p.m. Winter:
open Tue.–Sat. 10 a.m.–5 p.m.; Sun.
noon–4 p.m.

GETTING THERE
Located between Ashland and
Jacksonville just off Highway 99.
Follow I-5 and county road signs for
Eden Valley Orchards and Rogue
Valley Wine Center.

WINERY HIGHLIGHTS
The Rogue Valley Wine Center
features award-winning EdenVale
Wines as well as other premium
southern Oregon wines, local
cheeses and chocolates.

3. Preheat the oven to 400°F. Remove the fat from the stock and discard. Bring the stock to a boil, then reduce the heat and simmer to reduce the liquid.

4. Combine the pepper, fennel seeds and kosher salt and use the mixture to season the legs and breasts. Roast the legs for 1 hour and pour off any excess fat. Add ¾ bottle of Syrah and enough stock to almost cover the legs. Continue roasting for an additional hour before removing the legs to a plate to rest. Put the braising liquid in a saucepan and continue to reduce to a sauce consistency, up to 15 minutes. Add the minced garlic, parsley and thyme to the sauce and set aside.

5. Sear the breasts skin side down in a hot pan, pouring off the fat as it accumulates. Cook the breasts, about 4–5 minutes on 1 side, then flip and cook 1–2 minutes on the other. Remove to a plate and let rest for 5 minutes. Serve with the legs and top with the sauce. Enjoy with a glass of EdenVale Syrah.

SERVES 4–8

Honeywood Sweet and Sour Apricot Chicken

featuring HONEYWOOD APRICOT SUPREME WINE

½ cup apricot wine

¼ cup ketchup

¼ cup water

1 cup dried apricots, cut in strips

½ cup teriyaki sauce

1 tsp grated fresh ginger

1 tsp crushed garlic

2 Tbsp cornstarch

1 whole chicken, cut up

2 Tbsp sesame seeds

¼ cup sliced green onion for garnish

The classic combination of fruit and chicken could not be better displayed than with this simple recipe using Honeywood's Apricot Supreme Wine. Drier than most fruit wines, it's fresh and natural, with the juice of fully ripe apricots in perfect balance with a blend of quality white wine. Apricots are great with poultry and many seafood dishes.

1. Preheat the oven to 350°F. Combine the wine, ketchup, water, apricots, teriyaki sauce, ginger, garlic and cornstarch. Mix well to dissolve the cornstarch.

2. Place the chicken in an ovenproof dish and coat well with the sauce mixture. Sprinkle the top of the chicken with the sesame seeds.

3. Bake for 50–60 minutes until the top is bubbly and brown and the chicken has cooked through. Garnish with sliced green onion and serve with your choice of Honeywood wines. Of course, the apricot goes especially well!

SERVES 4

HONEYWOOD WINERY
1350 Hines Street SE, Salem
TEL: (503) 362-4111
FAX: (503) 362-4112
www.honeywoodwinery.com
info@honeywoodwinery.com

WINE SHOP, TOURS AND TASTINGS
Tasting room open Mon.-Fri. 9 a.m.-
5 p.m.; Sat. 10 a.m.-5 p.m. and Sun.
1 p.m.-5 p.m.

GETTING THERE
The winery is located just half a block
from 13th Street.

WINERY HIGHLIGHTS
Founded in 1933 as Columbia
Distillers, Honeywood is recognized
as the oldest winery in Oregon.

Fruit Wine

It is possible to create wine from just about anything that contains sugar or natural starch. This means just about any type of fruit can be turned into wine. In Oregon winemakers have been producing fruit wines for a long time. In fact, the state's longest-running winery, Honeywood, was set up by Ron Honeyman and John Wood the very day after prohibition ended in 1933. Fruit wines that are still produced at Honeywood include blackberry, raspberry, cranberry, loganberry, plum and rhubarb.

Serious wine consumers and winemakers alike are discovering that this type of wine has a lot to offer, and many conventional wineries are now adding fruit wines to their repertoire. One of the great things about fruit wines is that they're easy to understand. Usually a raspberry wine will taste like raspberries, a blueberry wine like blueberries. Many people find this makes them easier to pair with food, for both drinking and cooking, because they are already familiar with the flavors.

If you've never tried a fruit wine, or haven't tried one recently, head out to one of the wineries and sample some of their wares. You'll be pleasantly surprised by what you find.

Orchard Heights Easy Chicken Pinot Gris

featuring ORCHARD HEIGHTS PINOT GRIS

½ cup all-purpose flour

4–5 lb boneless, skinless
   chicken thighs or breasts

2 Tbsp oil

1 bottle Pinot Gris

2 tsp dried basil

You can just let the chicken simmer while you visit with your guests, and they'll think you spent hours preparing it. Elegant, easy and delicious.

1. Lightly flour the chicken pieces. Heat the oil in a large frying pan over medium-high heat and add the chicken. Brown the chicken on all sides, 4–5 minutes.

2. Remove the fat, leaving the chicken in the frying pan. Slowly pour the wine over the chicken and add the basil. Stir slightly and turn the chicken over once to distribute the basil.

3. Cook over medium-high heat until the sauce begins to bubble. Reduce the heat and simmer uncovered until the chicken is cooked through and the sauce has thickened, about 30 minutes.

4. Serve the chicken over your favorite rice. Crack open another bottle of Orchard Heights Pinot Gris and you have the perfect accompaniment.

SERVES 4–6

ORCHARD HEIGHTS WINERY
6057 Orchard Heights Road NW
Salem
TEL: (503) 391-7308
www.orchardheightswinery.com
info@orchardheightswinery.com

WINE SHOP, TOURS AND TASTINGS
Open daily except Thanksgiving,
Christmas and New Year's Day.
Mon.–Sat. 11 a.m.–5 p.m. and Sun.
9 a.m.–5 p.m. Sunday brunch is
served 9 a.m.–2 p.m.

GETTING THERE
From Salem, cross the Marion Street
Bridge and go 6 miles west on
Highway 22 toward Dallas, Ocean
Beaches. Turn right onto Oak Grove
Road. Go 2 miles and turn right onto
Orchard Heights Road. Just ahead,
turn left at the Orchard Heights
Winery sign.

WINERY HIGHLIGHTS
The winery is located in a park-like
setting, with gift shop, wine tastings,
daily food specials and Sunday
brunch. The brunch is reasonably
priced and features omelet and pasta
bars, waffles, biscuits and gravy,
cheese, fruit, breads, coffee, juice
and more.

WINERY SPECIAL OFFER
If you show your copy of this
book, you'll receive a complimentary
wine tasting.

Scott Paul Braised Chicken with Morels

featuring WHITE WINE AND SCOTT PAUL PINOT NOIR

2 Tbsp butter

1 Tbsp olive oil

8 cloves garlic, peeled

4 lb chicken thighs and legs (or a 3- or 4-lb chicken cut in pieces)

salt and freshly ground black pepper to taste

2 carrots, cut into 1-inch pieces

4 shallots, peeled and quartered

4 oz morels, rinsed well

1 sprig fresh thyme

⅔ cup dry white wine

2 cups low-sodium chicken stock (or rabbit stock if using rabbit)

½ lemon

Here in Oregon we are privileged to have access to an amazing array of wild mushrooms and truffles. This brings out the best in the morels and the Pinot. An unusual twist: white wine is used in the preparation, but the earthiness of the dish pairs wonderfully with Scott Paul Pinot Noir. You can substitute rabbit for the chicken; choose a 2- or 3-pound rabbit and cook it a little longer.

1. Heat 1 Tbsp of the butter and the oil in a large casserole or deep frying pan over medium-high heat.

2. Add the garlic and sauté for 2–3 minutes. Transfer to a plate. Add the chicken to the pan and brown for about 3 minutes per side. Season well with salt and pepper.

3. Transfer the chicken to a plate, pour off any fat and reduce the heat to medium-low. Add the carrots and shallots and allow to cook for about 10 minutes or until they're soft and beginning to brown. Add the morels and thyme and cook for another minute or two.

SCOTT PAUL WINES
128 South Pine Street, Carlton
TEL: (503) 274-4700
www.scottpaul.com
kellykarr@scottpaul.com

WINE SHOP, TOURS AND TASTINGS
Tasting room open Wed.-Sun.
11 a.m.-4 p.m. Private tours by
appointment. A small tasting fee
(generally $5) covers current
release Scott Paul wines and a flight
of Burgundies from small family
domaines imported under the Scott
Paul Selections division.

GETTING THERE
From Route 99W just north of
McMinnville, take Route 47 north
toward Carlton for 5 miles. The winery
is on the right just before you reach
Main Street in downtown Carlton.

WINERY HIGHLIGHTS
The winery is devoted exclusively to
the production of Oregon Pinot Noir.
Many of the vineyards use organic,
sustainable growing practices (see
LIVE, page 19).

4. Return the garlic and chicken to the pan and increase the heat to medium-high. Add the wine and simmer until the wine has reduced by half, scraping up any browned bits on the bottom of the pan. Add the stock and bring to a simmer. Cover the pot and cook until the meat is cooked through, about 15–20 minutes (20–30 minutes if using rabbit).

5. Remove the chicken and keep it warm. Spoon off any grease in the liquid, increase the heat and cook until the liquid is reduced by half. Add a squeeze of fresh lemon juice, swirl in the remaining 1 Tbsp of butter and adjust with salt and pepper, if desired. Return the meat to the pot, heat through and serve with a glass of Scott Paul Pinot Noir.

SERVES 6

WillaKenzie Roulade of Oregon Pheasant

featuring WILLAKENZIE ESTATE PINOT NOIR ALIETTE

1 whole pheasant (3–4 lb)

2 bay leaves

1 carrot, chopped

1 bunch fresh thyme

2 cups Pinot Noir

2 Tbsp soy sauce

2 Tbsp unsalted butter

4 Tbsp olive oil

1 medium leek, chopped,
   reserving 2 flat 3 × 3-inch
   squares

1 stalk celery, minced

1 shallot, minced

1 clove garlic, chopped

salt and freshly ground black
   pepper to taste

½ lb assorted fresh wild
   mushrooms (or 2 oz dried
   mushrooms, rehydrated)

1 lb porcini pasta, cooked

*Executive Chef Paul Bachand from La Rambla has come up
with this incredible recipe for pheasant roulade. Yes, it is
complicated, but the results are worth the effort. Pinot Noir
is a great match for pheasant as the meat is rich, yet the flavors
are delicate.*

1. Preheat the oven to 425°F. Remove the skin from the
   pheasant by running your fingers under the skin beginning
   at the tail end and moving forward. Be careful not to tear
   the skin. Set the skin aside for later use. Set the bird on its
   back with the breast facing up. Remove the breast meat by
   running a sharp knife along the top of the breastbone and
   separating the meat carefully from the carcass. The wings
   should still be attached to the breasts; this is called an
   "airline breast."

2. Remove the legs and thighs from the bird and cut away all
   the meat. Set aside to use for stuffing. Keep all the bones.
   Cut the second joint away from the wing bone, leaving a
   small "drummette."

3. Roast the bones and remaining carcass until lightly
   caramelized, about 20 minutes, then place in a medium
   stockpot and just cover with cold water. Add the bay
   leaves, carrot and thyme. Bring to just under a boil and
   cook for 1 hour at a low simmer. Strain and discard
   the solids. Add the Pinot Noir and soy sauce and cook
   over medium-high heat until reduced to half its original
   volume. Swirl in 1 Tbsp of the butter, set aside and
   keep warm.

4. Scrape the wing bones down to expose the bone and create
   a "frenched bone" (exposed bone with no meat attached).
   Lay the breasts with the skinned side down between
   2 sheets of plastic wrap. Cover with another sheet of
   plastic. Gently flatten the breasts with a meat mallet
   until they double in size.

WILLAKENZIE ESTATE VINEYARD
619143 NE Laughlin Road, Yamhill
TEL: (503) 662-3280
FAX: (503) 662-4829
www.willakenzie.com
winery@willakenzie.com

WINE SHOP, TOURS AND TASTINGS
May–Oct open daily, Nov.–Apr. open
Fri. and weekends or by appointment.
Hours are always noon–5 p.m.
Appointments required for groups of
more than 6.

GETTING THERE
From Newberg, turn right on Main
Street, which is also Highway 240W
signed Chehalem Valley, Yamhill.
Continue on Highway 240 about 10
miles to Laughlin Road. Turn right on
Laughlin Road. and continue about 1½
miles. WillaKenzie Estate is on the left.

WINERY HIGHLIGHTS
WillaKenzie focuses on the Pinot
varietals. The three-level design of
the winery allows gravity, not
mechanical pumps, to move the fruit
from vine to vintage.

5. Heat 1 Tbsp of the olive oil and sauté the chopped leek, celery, shallot and garlic until translucent, about 5 minutes. Set aside to cool. Meanwhile, grind the reserved leg and thigh meat in a food grinder or processor until well chopped. Add to the sautéed vegetable mixture.

6. Blanch the two 3- × 3-inch squares of green leek in a little salted water. Lay a leek piece out flat and place the ground meat mixture in the middle of the square. Roll up into a cigar shape and place it in the middle of the flattened breast. Roll the breast into a tight cylinder shape. Wrap the reserved skin around the breast and season with salt and pepper. Repeat with the other breast.

7. Sauté the mushrooms in 2 Tbsp of the olive oil over medium-high heat until lightly browned, about 5 minutes. Add 1 cup of the Pinot Noir sauce and slowly warm through; do not boil.

8. Heat the remaining 1 Tbsp of olive oil in a separate pan and add the remaining 1 Tbsp of butter. When it has melted, place the roulade with the seam side down over low heat. Cook on all sides until golden brown. Keep warm.

9. Slice each of the breasts on the bias into 4 pieces. Toss the pasta with the Pinot Noir/mushroom sauce. Twirl the pasta around a fork and place in the middle of a warm plate; arrange the roulade around the pasta and drizzle with the remaining sauce.

SERVES 4

Meat

Two times a week my wife and I go to
a nice restaurant for companionship, soft
music, dancing, good food and a little wine.
She goes on Tuesdays and I go on Fridays.

—Henny Youngman

Airlie Winery's Incredible Foch Lamb Shanks

featuring AIRLIE MARÉCHAL FOCH

1 Tbsp olive oil

4 lamb shanks

1 large onion, finely chopped

2 carrots, finely chopped

2 stalks celery, finely chopped

4 cloves garlic, crushed

2 Tbsp tomato paste

1 bottle Maréchal Foch

1 can beef broth (14 oz)

2 bay leaves

1 tsp dried thyme (or
   rosemary)

½ tsp black pepper

¼ cup chopped fresh parsley

Amazing color, medium-bodied tannins and a smooth mouth feel make this wine a delight. With blackcurrant to start and spices to finish it's easy to enjoy on its own, with roasts in the winter and with rich pasta dishes in the summer. Here it's incredible with tender lamb shanks braised in a wine sauce.

1. Preheat the oven to 325°F. Heat the oil over high heat in a large heavy Dutch oven and brown the lamb shanks for 2–3 minutes. Remove the shanks and lower the heat to medium.

2. Add the onion, carrots, celery and garlic and sauté 5–6 minutes or until softened. Add the tomato paste and sauté 1–2 minutes more.

3. Return the lamb to the pan along with the wine, broth, bay leaves, thyme and pepper. Make sure the lamb is covered with the liquid. Bring to a boil and place in the oven. Braise for 2½–3 hours. When done, remove the shanks carefully as the meat will fall off the bones.

4. Skim the fat from the top of the sauce. Reduce the sauce on the stovetop over medium-high heat until it reaches your desired consistency and taste. Add the parsley just before serving.

5. This is great over bow tie noodles. We like to put the noodles in the bottom of a big bowl, arrange the shanks on top and pour the sauce over the entire dish! Serve with a glass of Airlie Maréchal Foch, of course, as it's a perfect match!

SERVES 4

AIRLIE WINERY AND DUNN FOREST
VINEYARD

15305 Dunn Forest Road, Monmouth
TEL: (503) 838-6013
FAX: (503) 838-6364
www.airliewinery.com
airlie@airliewinery.com

WINE SHOP, TOURS AND TASTINGS
Open weekends Mar.-Dec. noon-
5 p.m. or other times by appointment.
They love to share their passion for
wine and give tours when possible.

GETTING THERE
20 miles north of Corvallis, 12 miles
south of Monmouth. Take 99W
6 miles south of Monmouth to Airlie
Road. Six miles west on Airlie Road
turn left on Maxfield Creek Road and
follow the signs.

WINERY HIGHLIGHTS
Established in 1986, Airlie Winery
and Dunn Forest Vineyard is a
destination winery and the view
alone is well worth the trip. Pack a
picnic and your pooch and enjoy a
day in the countryside!

WINERY SPECIAL OFFER
Show your copy of this book and you
will receive a souvenir wine glass
worthy of their great reds!

Maréchal Foch

pronounced (Mah-reh-shal Fohsh)

"Victory is a thing of the will," exclaimed General Ferdinand Foch, a famous French field marshal and commander of the Allied forces during World War I. A French hybridizer called Eugene Kuhlman was greatly impressed by the actions of General Foch and named this grape after him.

The full name of the grape is Maréchal Foch, although it is sometimes shortened to Foch. It is an early ripening, high-tonnage grape that is able to withstand harsh winter conditions. It was first grown in the United States during the 1940s and was once very popular in the eastern states.

It has recently become a very fashionable wine in Oregon and is often compared to Lemberger. Maréchal Foch can have characteristics of chocolate, coffee and blackcurrant and is usually dark and rich in color. It goes well with roasted meat, duck, lamb, rich pasta dishes and even game. It's well worth making the effort to find this wine. It's sometimes predicted to be the next "big thing" in Oregon reds.

Carlovanna Vineyards Marionberry Glazed Ham

featuring Carlovanna Vineyards Marionberry Wine

½ cup brown sugar

⅓ cup orange juice

¼ tsp allspice

½ cup marionberry wine

½ ham, spiral-sliced (7–9 lb)

fresh marionberries for garnish

2 oranges, thinly sliced, for garnish

This wine, named "Amore di Angeli" (Angels' Love), was crafted using centuries-old Italian winemaking techniques and fruit grown in the fertile soils of Oregon's Willamette Valley. This easy recipe would be perfect for a Christmas or Thanksgiving feast.

1. Preheat the oven to 300°F. Combine the brown sugar, orange juice and allspice in a small saucepan. Bring to a boil and simmer for 5 minutes. Add the wine and simmer for 1 minute.

2. Place the ham on a baking tray. Drizzle half the wine syrup over the ham, using a spoon to lift each slice and pour glaze in between the slices.

3. Bake 14–18 minutes per pound, basting occasionally. When a meat thermometer reaches 130°F the meat is done.

4. Remove the ham from the oven and transfer to a serving platter. Drizzle with the remaining glaze and garnish with fresh marionberries and thinly sliced oranges.

Serves 10

CARLOVANNA VINEYARD
7575 Heron Street, Salem
TEL: (503) 779-7584
www.carlovanna.com
customerservice@carlovanna.com

WINE SHOP, TOURS AND TASTINGS
Tastings by appointment only. Please
call or email in advance.

GETTING THERE
The winery is located between
Salem and Silverton about 1 hour
south of Portland.

WINERY HIGHLIGHTS
Premium fruit wines are made in
the Italian tradition with Oregon's
finest fruit.

WINERY SPECIAL OFFER
If you show your copy of this book
you'll receive a 10 percent discount
on your purchase.

Chateau Bianca Pork Loins Pinot Blanc

featuring CHATEAU BIANCA PINOT BLANC

4 pork loins

salt and freshly ground black
pepper to taste

2 Tbsp olive oil

2 firm ripe pears, cored, peeled
and sliced

½ cup Pinot Blanc

1 Tbsp grated lemon zest

1 Tbsp chopped chives

This incredibly simple recipe produces delightful results. The Pinot Blanc is an excellent wine match for pork, which in turn is a great match for the sweetness of the pears. The Chateau Bianca Pinot Blanc has pretty pear and melon aromas. Fermented in cool temperature conditions, the delicate flavors are captured on the palate. The soft, round mid-palate finishes with a touch of citrus.

1. Pound the pork loins using a meat mallet (or rolling pin covered in plastic wrap) until they are flattened to ½ inch thick. Generously salt and pepper each side of the pork loins.

2. Heat 1 Tbsp of the oil in a heavy pan over medium-high heat. Brown both sides of the pork, about 2–3 minutes. Remove the meat from the pan. Add the remaining 1 Tbsp of oil and brown the pears, about 2–3 minutes. Remove them from the pan.

3. Add the wine and use a wooden spoon to scrape up any browned bits from the bottom of the pan. Add the lemon zest and chives and allow the sauce to reduce slightly, about 4–5 minutes.

4. To serve, arrange the loins and pears on a platter and pour the sauce over. Complete the meal with rice and salad. Enjoy with a glass of Chateau Bianca Pinot Blanc.

SERVES 4

CHATEAU BIANCA
17485 Highway 22, Dallas
TEL: (503) 623-6181
www.chateaubianca.com
chateaubianca@qwest.net

WINE SHOP, TOURS AND TASTINGS
Tastings daily Oct.–May, 11 a.m.–
5 p.m. and Jun.–Sep. 10 a.m.–6 p.m.
Tours by appointment. Closed
during Jan.

GETTING THERE
The winery is 20 minutes west of
Salem on Highway 22.

WINERY HIGHLIGHTS
The real highlight is the great
selection of varietal wines, but
you might also like to stay in the
fabulous bed and breakfast onsite.
There is also an RV turnaround and
picnic facility.

Pinot Blanc

pronounced (PEE-NO-BLAHN)

*Pinot Blanc is sometimes unfairly referred to as
the poor man's Chardonnay. This comment is unfair
because when it's done right the wine rivals even the
best Chardonnay.*

*Pinot Blanc is a mutation of Pinot Gris, which itself
is a mutation of the Pinot Noir variety. The grape is
thought to have originated in the Burgundy region of
France, but it's now predominantly grown in the Alsace
region. The grape looks so much like Chardonnay
that in some vineyards in Europe the two varieties
are intermingled.*

*The first Oregon Pinot Blanc appeared on the market in
the late 1980s. There are now large plantings of Pinot
Blanc throughout the state, especially in the Willamette
Valley, where the grape seems to do very well. There are
also some new Pinot Blanc clones that result in grapes
with higher sugar levels and reduced acidity.*

*Common characteristics of the wine include aromas of
apple, vanilla, almonds and hazelnuts. This wine pairs
well with seafood, light pastas and pork. It also makes
a great aperitif when served with olives and cheese.*

RoxyAnn Winery Roast Rib of Beef

featuring RoxyAnn Claret

1 beef rib roast (5–6 lb)

1 tsp each salt and pepper

1 bottle red wine

6 cups demi-glace

8 black peppercorns

3 Tbsp tomato paste

3 cloves

½ cup chopped shallots

6 sprigs fresh thyme

¼ lb unsalted butter, cut into
   small pieces

Chef David Taub at the Chateaulin Restaurant in Ashland is a great friend of the RoxyAnn Winery and this dish features the RoxyAnn Claret. The wine is a dark plush blend of Merlot, Cabernet Sauvignon and Cabernet Franc with layers of ripe currant, black cherry and blackberry fruit flavors. Chef Taub is famous for his elegant sauces. If you can't get this much demi-glace, use the best quality stock you can find.

1. Preheat the oven to 450°F. Rub the roast with the salt and pepper and place on a rack in a roasting pan, fat side up. Cook 45 minutes, then reduce the heat to 325°F. Continue cooking another 45 minutes, or until a meat thermometer indicates an internal temperature of 120°F for rare, 127°F for medium rare or 135°F for medium. Remove the roast from the oven and let it rest, covered loosely with foil, for 20 minutes.

2. While the roast is cooking, make the sauce. Combine all the remaining ingredients except the butter in a deep saucepan and slowly reduce over medium heat until the sauce coats the back of a spoon, about 1–1½ hours. Whisk in the butter 1 piece at a time until it's all incorporated.

3. Slice the beef and pour the wine sauce overtop. Open another bottle of RoxyAnn Claret and enjoy the meal with your guests.

Serves 8–10

ROXYANN WINERY
3285 Hillcrest Road, Medford
TEL: (541) 776-2315
FAX: (541) 245-1840
www.roxyann.com
michael@roxyann.com

WINE SHOP, TOURS AND TASTINGS
Open daily 11 a.m.–6 p.m. Many
wines are available to taste for a
nominal fee.

GETTING THERE
Located just minutes off I-5, exit
27 in Medford, Oregon. Travel east
on Barnett Road. Turn left on North
Phoenix Road, and left again on
Hillcrest Road.

WINERY HIGHLIGHTS
Visitors are encouraged to bring a
picnic and do some wine tasting
while enjoying the beautiful gardens
overlooking the vineyard. The tasting
room is in the historic Hillcrest
barn. Varietals include Cabernet
Sauvignon, Malbec, Merlot, Cabernet
Franc, Grenache, Tempranillo,
Viognier and Syrah.

Cherry Hill's Venison Medallions with Sun-Dried Berry Demi-Glace

featuring CHERRY HILL ESTATE PINOT NOIR

1 lb venison tenderloin, trimmed (at room temperature)

1 tsp kosher salt

1 tsp freshly ground black pepper

1 Tbsp olive oil

2 Tbsp unsalted butter

½ cup finely chopped shallots

1 cup Pinot Noir

1 cup beef or veal demi-glace

1 cup sun-dried berries, coarsely chopped (strawberries are great)

The elegant Cherry Hill Estate Pinot Noir has lively flavors of raspberry and plum. It complements the rich, earthy flavors of venison and the berry demi-glace. Chef Kjeld Peterson of Wild Plum Catering in Portland is a frequent guest at Cherry Hill Wine Camp, and he's served this dish at the James Beard House in NYC and at Cherry Hill.

1. Preheat the oven to 425°F. Pat the venison dry and rub in the salt and pepper.

2. Heat the oil and 1 Tbsp of the butter over medium-high heat in an ovenproof, 12-inch heavy frying pan until just smoking. Add the venison and brown all sides, about 3 minutes total.

3. Transfer the frying pan to the oven and roast until a meat thermometer inserted in the center of the meat reads 120°F, 8–12 minutes. Transfer the venison to a plate and let it stand, loosely covered with aluminum foil. The temperature will rise to 125°F for medium rare.

4. While the meat stands, add the shallots to the frying pan (be careful as the handle will be hot!) and cook over medium heat, stirring until golden, about 2 minutes.

CHERRY HILL WINERY

7867 Crowley Road, Rickreall

TEL: (503) 623-7867

FAX: (503) 623-7878

www.cherryhillwinery.com

info@cherryhillwinery.com

WINE SHOP, TOURS AND TASTINGS

Tasting room open weekends May 1–
Oct. 1 and Thanksgiving weekend
11 a.m.–5 p.m. Open other times by
appointment. The Guest Camp is
open Memorial weekend to Oct. 1.

GETTING THERE

Located just 1 hour south of
Portland and 15 minutes west of
Salem, the winery is just north of
Highway 22. There are Cherry Hill
Winery signs marking the way from
Highway 22 and the first turn is onto
Oak Grove Road.

WINERY HIGHLIGHTS

Experience Oregon's wine country
in a new way by visiting the Guest
Camp. You can cultivate your
palate with wine and food at the
one-of-a-kind viticultural dude
ranch in the Eola Hills region of the
Willamette Valley.

WINERY SPECIAL OFFER

If you show your copy of this book,
you'll receive a souvenir wine glass
with your tasting.

5. Increase the heat to high, add the wine and deglaze by boiling and scraping up any browned bits. The liquid should reduce by about half in 1–2 minutes. Add the demi-glace and boil, stirring until the sauce is slightly thickened, about 1–2 minutes. Stir in the berries, the remaining 1 Tbsp butter and any meat juices that have accumulated in the pan. Remove from the heat. Adjust the seasoning with salt and pepper to taste.

6. Cut the venison into ½-inch-thick slices and serve with berry sauce drizzled over and around the slices. At James Beard House this dish was served with a pearl couscous risotto, quince paste and crisped, thickly sliced, pork belly bacon.

Serves 4

Bridget's Baked Pasta Dry Hollow-Style

featuring DRY HOLLOW'S FT. DALLES RED

3 Tbsp extra virgin olive oil

1 lb Italian cooked ham, cut into ½-inch cubes

1 small carrot, diced

1 onion, diced

1 stalk celery, thinly sliced

1 cup dry red wine

1½ cups tomato sauce

1½ lb ziti (long thin tubes of macaroni)

1 lb fresh ricotta

8 oz hard provolone, diced

½ cup freshly grated Parmigiano Reggiano

Mediterranean sea salt (Bela Mandil Flor de Sal) and freshly ground black pepper to taste

The real name of this recipe is "Pasticcio di Maccheroni," which the author of this recipe (Bridget) translates as "One Beautiful Mess." The recipe was created using the Ft. Dalles Red, which is a Merlot, Cabernet Sauvignon and Syrah blend. The Merlot and Syrah are grown on the south-facing Hi Valley Vineyard on Dry Hollow Lane in The Dalles. The wine is oaky, with a light fruit taste and smooth finish.

1. Heat the olive oil over high heat in a Dutch oven. Add the ham cubes and brown for 5 minutes. Season with salt and pepper. Add the carrot, onion and celery and cook until the vegetables are golden brown, about 10 minutes.

2. Add the wine, bring to a boil and cook until reduced by half, about 5 minutes. Add the tomato sauce and bring to a boil. Reduce the heat to low, cover the pan and cook until the meat is just about falling apart, about 50 minutes. Transfer to a large bowl and keep the sauce warm.

3. Preheat the oven to 450°F. Grease a 12-inch deep round casserole or pie dish with olive oil and set aside. Bring a large pot of water to a boil and add 2 Tbsp salt.

4. Cook the ziti in the boiling water for 1 minute less than package directions, until very *al dente*. While the pasta is cooking, place the ricotta in a small bowl and stir in a ladle of the pasta cooking water.

DRY HOLLOW VINEYARDS
3410 Dry Hollow Lane, The Dalles
TEL: (541) 296-2953
www.dryhollowvineyards.com
bridget@dryhollowvineyards.com

WINE SHOP, TOURS AND TASTINGS
Open Memorial Day weekend
through to Thanksgiving, Fri.–Sun.,
noon–5 p.m. or by appointment.

GETTING THERE
From I-84 take exit 85. Go right onto
Highway 30. Take a sharp right and
head up Brewery Grade. Continue
on Dry Hollow Road for 3 miles. Turn
right onto Dry Hollow Lane.

WINERY HIGHLIGHTS
The tasting room is nestled in a
cherry orchard.

WINERY SPECIAL OFFER
Show your copy of this book for a
complimentary wine tasting.

5. Drain the pasta and add it to the bowl with the meat sauce. Mix in the ricotta and provolone, then transfer the mixture to the prepared casserole. Sprinkle half the grated cheese overtop.

6. Bake for 25 minutes, until bubbling and heated through. Serve in warmed pasta bowls. Pass around the remaining grated cheese. Accompany with a glass of Fort Dalles Red. Salud! If you're feeding a smaller crowd, this dish freezes well.

SERVES 6–8

Firesteed's Pork Loin Roast

featuring FIRESTEED PINOT GRIS

3 cloves garlic, crushed

1 Tbsp dried rosemary

½ tsp salt

½ tsp freshly ground black pepper

3 Tbsp fresh lemon juice

3 Tbsp olive oil

1 boneless pork loin (3-4 lb)

1 cup Pinot Gris

Firesteed Pinot Gris combines delicate floral aromas with rich tropical fruit. The fresh acidity of the north balances the ripe, full texture of the south. Flavors of orange blossom, honeysuckle, pineapple, papaya, poached pear and mandarin orange linger on the palate and it has a refreshing finish with hints of spice and melon. All of this makes it the perfect wine for pork roast.

1. Preheat the oven to 325°F. In a small bowl combine the garlic, rosemary, salt, pepper, lemon juice and oil.

2. Place the pork loin in a roasting pan just slightly larger than the roast and pour the marinade over the meat. Rub it in, ensuring all the meat is covered. Roast in the oven for 20 minutes per pound of meat.

3. Remove the meat to a platter and keep it warm. Place the roasting pan over medium heat and use a wooden spoon to scrape any brown bits from the bottom of the pan. Cook for 4–5 minutes, then pour the sauce over the sliced meat.

4. Serve with your choice of vegetables and, of course, a glass of Firesteed Pinot Gris.

SERVES 4–6

FIRESTEED CELLARS

2200 North Pacific Highway West
Rickreall
TEL: (503) 623-8683
www.firesteed.com
cspagna@firesteed.com

WINE SHOP, TOURS AND TASTINGS
Tasting room open daily 11 a.m.–5 p.m.
Large groups or private tours by
appointment.

GETTING THERE
Firesteed Cellars is located 13 miles
west of Salem. It is on Pacific
Highway 99W just 2 miles north
of Highway 22.

WINERY HIGHLIGHTS
Taste an array of award-winning
wines while overlooking a beautiful
view of the heart of the Willamette
Valley.

Holloran Riesling Pork Tenderloin

featuring HOLLORAN "LE PAVILLON VINEYARD" RIESLING

2 dried apricots, chopped

1 dried pear half, chopped

½ cup hot water

4 Tbsp unsalted butter, softened

2 tsp minced fresh rosemary

2 cloves garlic, minced

twist of ground black pepper

2 pork tenderloins (1½ lb each)

2 Tbsp olive oil

6 slices prosciutto

1¾ cups Riesling

Holloran Le Pavillon Riesling is grown on volcanic Jory soil in the Dundee Hills, and is made from vines planted over 30 years ago. It offers aromas of dried pear, citrus and fresh peaches, with a broad mid-palate and a long, balanced finish. Its bright acidity and flavorful fruit profile make it a good match for this pork dish.

1. Preheat the oven to 375°F. Soak the fruit in the hot water for 30 minutes. Drain and reserve the liquid.

2. Mix 2 Tbsp of the butter with the rosemary, garlic and pepper in a small bowl. Pat the tenderloins dry and make four 1-inch slits, halfway through on the topside of the pork. Stuff the butter mixture into the slits. Heat the olive oil over medium heat in an ovenproof baking dish (we use a copper gratin pan). Sear all sides of the tenderloins for 4–6 minutes per side until golden brown, then remove from the heat to a work surface.

3. Wrap 3 slices of prosciutto around each tenderloin. Tie the tenderloins in several places with kitchen string. Return them to the baking dish and add 1 cup of the Riesling, half of the fruit and all of the fruit liquid. Roast until a meat thermometer inserted into the thickest part of the meat reads 140°F, usually between 45 and 60 minutes. Baste frequently throughout the cooking process, and add ½ cup of the wine directly over the meat when needed.

HOLLORAN VINEYARD WINES

2636 SW Schaeffer Road, West Linn

TEL: (503) 638-6224

FAX: (503) 638-3680

www.holloranwine.com

bill@holloranvineyardwines.com

WINE SHOP, TOURS AND TASTINGS
Open for tasting and tours year round
by appointment. Open to the public
Sun.–Mon. of Memorial Day weekend
and Fri.–Sat. of Thanksgiving
weekend. A $3 tasting fee is refunded
with your purchase.

GETTING THERE
From I-205 take exit 3 to Stafford
Road. Proceed south on Stafford Road
¾ mile, then turn left on Mountain
Road and take the third left onto
Schaeffer Road.

WINERY HIGHLIGHTS
HVW produces small quantities of
hand-crafted Pinot Noir, Riesling and
Chardonnay from premium vineyard
sites in Oregon's Willamette Valley.
They emphasize low yields and
careful hands-on management of the
vines to produce wines that express
the unique characteristics of their
vineyard sites.

4. Remove the meat from the pan and wrap loosely in foil. Let it rest for 15 minutes. This is where the meat completes the cooking process.

5. Begin preparation of the sauce by melting the remaining 2 Tbsp of butter over medium heat. Add the remaining ¼ cup of Riesling, 1 tsp of the pan juice and the reserved fruit. Simmer for 2–3 minutes and remove from the heat.

6. Remove the string from the tenderloins and cut the meat into ½-inch slices. Arrange the meat on individual plates and drizzle the sauce overtop. Serve with a glass of Holloran "Le Pavillon Vineyard" Riesling.

SERVES 6

Marquam Hill Vineyards Venison with Blue Cheese and Raspberries

featuring MARQUAM HILL VINEYARDS PINOT NOIR

16 small red potatoes, scrubbed and the skins partially removed

¼ cup olive oil

2 Tbsp chopped cilantro

8 Tbsp butter

4 venison rib-eye steaks (½–¾ inch thick)

1½ cups Pinot Noir

¼ cup crumbled blue cheese

1 handful fresh red raspberries

½ lb baby carrots

2 Tbsp chopped fresh dill

Winemaker Joe Dobbes has shared his favorite venison recipe. The wine has a bouquet of blackcurrant and black raspberries, followed by hints of leather and pepper and finishing with a lingering hint of anise. Pair with lamb, venison or a slow-roasted prime rib. You might taste a bit of heaven if you pair it with a chocolate raspberry truffle.

1. Preheat the oven to 350°F. Lightly coat the potatoes with olive oil in a roasting pan and sprinkle with 1 Tbsp of the cilantro. Roast in the oven until golden and crispy, about 30 minutes.

2. Melt 3 Tbsp of the butter with a drizzle of olive oil in a frying pan over medium-high heat. Brown each side of the steaks. Continue to cook to medium-rare, about 3–4 minutes each side. Set the meat aside and cover with foil to keep warm.

3. Add the Pinot Noir to the pan and use a wooden spoon to scrape up any browned bits from the bottom. Add another 3 Tbsp of the butter and the crumbled blue cheese. Add the raspberries and continue to stir until everything is well combined and the sauce is starting to reduce. Turn the heat to low, return the venison to the pan and allow to heat through.

4. Heat the remaining 2 Tbsp butter in a separate frying pan over medium-high heat and sauté the carrots until fork tender, about 8 minutes. Sprinkle with the dill.

5. Plate the steaks with the sauce pooled below and drizzled overtop. Add the carrots and potatoes and sprinkle the remaining 1 Tbsp fresh cilantro over the potatoes. Serve with a bottle of Marquam Hill Pinot Noir.

SERVES 4

MARQUAM HILL VINEYARDS

35803 South Highway 213, Molalla

TEL: (503) 829-6677

FAX: (503) 829-8810

www.marquamhillvineyards.biz

marquam@molalla.net

WINE SHOP, TOURS AND TASTINGS

Tasting room is open Tue.–Sun.
10 a.m.–5 p.m. in winter and 10 a.m.–
6 p.m. in summer. Closed in Jan.

GETTING THERE

From I-5 take exit 271, Woodburn
exit. Follow Highway 211 for 20
minutes to the junction of 213.
From the junction follow the signs for
5 miles to Marquam Hill Vineyard.

WINERY HIGHLIGHTS

An 8-acre lake surrounded by
timberland provides a serene setting
for visitors to enjoy a family outing,
picnic, wedding, reunion, concert or
corporate event.

Pinot Noir

pronounced (PEE-NO-NWAHR)

The Pinot Noir grape has been used to make wine since at least the first century AD. Ancient Romans called the grape Helvenacia Minor. The grape is most famous because of the wines produced in the Burgundy region of France; however, many wine experts claim the world's best Pinot Noir comes from Oregon.

David Lett of Eyrie Vineyards often gets credit for the rise of Pinot Noir and, indeed, the entire wine industry in Oregon. He first planted the varietal in the mid-1960s, but captured the attention of the global press in 1979 during a huge wine competition in Paris when his Pinot Noir placed third in the entire world.

Wine judges could not believe this was possible and a rematch with more experienced judges was scheduled. The very next year his wine placed second, less than half a point behind the famous 1959 Drohin Chambelle-Musigny. The legacy of Oregon's world-beating Pinot Noir had begun. After witnessing first-hand the amazing Oregon wine, French winemaker Robert Drohin set up a winery of his own only a hop, skip and a jump from Lett's Eyrie vineyard.

(CONTINUED ON NEXT PAGE)

Pinot Noir (CONT'D)

Pinot Noir has not achieved the worldwide popularity of some other reds. This may be because its overall quality is generally a little more inconsistent: it's known as one of the toughest grapes to grow and to turn into wine. This is rarely a problem for the excellent Oregon Pinot Noirs. The film **Sideways** *boosted Pinot Noir sales, and when it's done right, Pinot Noir is many wine lovers' favorite tipple.*

Pinot Noir can have many different characteristics, but some common ones include flavors and aromas of raspberry, cherry, rose petals, oregano and rhubarb. The wine is generally believed to be at its best five to eight years after the vintage.

This wine is wonderful with a wide variety of foods. Some great pairings are salmon, tuna, lamb, chicken, pork, smoked meats, hearty stews, wild mushrooms and duck.

Chardonnay Sausages

featuring CHARDONNAY

Sausages do not have to be boring! This is something Europeans have always known and this recipe brings a little of that to the table. The tasty sauce works just as well with your standard grocery store sausage as it does with the gourmet butcher type. If you are using very lean sausages you don't need to cook them for quite as long, so add them to the pan a little later.

2 lb sausages

2 Tbsp butter

1 Tbsp all-purpose flour

2½ cups Chardonnay

1 bay leaf

2 shallots, finely chopped

½ tsp dried marjoram

salt and freshly ground black pepper to taste

2 Tbsp chopped fresh flat-leaf parsley

1. Prick the sausages so they don't burst while cooking. (This is why the English refer to sausages as bangers.)

2. Brown the sausages in a large non-stick frying pan over medium-high heat. This should take 4–5 minutes. Remove the sausages and drain the fat from the pan.

3. Add the butter to the pan and melt it over medium heat. Add the flour and stir well to form a roux, about 2–3 minutes. Add the wine slowly, stirring constantly. Add the bay leaf, shallots and marjoram and bring the sauce to a boil. Allow to simmer for about 15 minutes.

4. Put the sausages back in the pan and allow them to cook through, about 15–20 minutes. The sauce should be thickened. Season with salt and pepper. Garnish with the parsley.

5. This dish is absolutely fantastic served over creamed potatoes. It also goes well with crusty bread and an omelet.

SERVES 6

Oak Knoll Pacific Rim Lamb

featuring OAK KNOLL PINOT NOIR

2 cups Pinot Noir

½ cup olive oil

⅓ cup soy sauce

1 Tbsp minced garlic

2 Tbsp grated fresh ginger

1 tsp cumin

1 tsp freshly ground black
  pepper

Oregon leg of lamb, boned and
  butterflied (6 lb)

This wine exhibits a dark garnet color and aromas of cherry, cloves and leather. On the palate the wine is supple and round, with flavors of berry and cinnamon spice framed by supple notes of vanilla and smoky oak. The wine possesses mouth-watering acidity, with spice and berry in the lingering finish. The acidity makes it a suitable match for lamb, and it would also hold up well against a tomato-based pasta dish.

1. Combine the wine, oil, soy sauce, garlic, ginger, cumin and pepper in a non-metallic dish. Add the lamb and turn to coat it well. Cover, refrigerate and marinate for 6–12 hours. Turn occasionally to ensure all parts of the meat are marinated.

2. Broil in the oven or grill on the barbecue 5–6 inches from the heat source until the lamb reaches the desired doneness, about 45 minutes for medium rare. Baste with the marinade throughout the cooking process. Remove from the heat and allow the meat to rest for 15 minutes before carving.

3. Serve with small red oven-roasted potatoes tossed with melted butter and chopped rosemary, a salad of your choice and a glass of Oak Knoll Pinot Noir.

SERVES 6–8

OAK KNOLL WINERY

29700 SW Burkhalter Road, Hilsboro

TEL: (503) 648-8198

FAX: (503) 648-3377

www.oakknollwinery.com

info@oakknollwinery.com

WINE SHOP, TOURS AND TASTINGS

Tasting room is open daily Mar.–Sep., Mon.–Fri. 11 a.m.–6 p.m. and 11 a.m.–5 p.m. on weekends. From Oct.–Apr. hours are 11 a.m.–5 p.m. daily. There is no charge for tasting.

GETTING THERE

On Highway 219, 4 miles south of downtown Hilsboro, turn left onto Burkhalter Road. Go ½ mile to the stop sign. Burkhalter Road continues to the right; go another ¼ mile and the winery is on your right.

WINERY HIGHLIGHTS

The winery is almost 40 years old and is now run by the second generation of the Vuylsteke family. Check the website for information about the summer concert series and other events.

Stoller Vineyard's Braised Short Ribs

featuring STOLLER VINEYARD PINOT NOIR

3–4 lb beef short ribs

3 onions, cut into chunks

3 stalks celery, cut into slices

2 heads garlic, cut in half horizontally

1 Tbsp black peppercorns

1 oz dried mushrooms (porcini, morels or cepes preferred)

6 cups Pinot Noir

sea salt and freshly ground black pepper to taste

2 cups all-purpose flour

¼ cup olive oil

1 bouquet garni (fresh sprigs of thyme, oregano, Italian parsley and rosemary tied together)

2 bay leaves

1 can Italian stewed tomatoes (14 oz)

3 cups unsalted chicken or beef stock

Cathy Stoller says: "This dish requires a little planning ahead and although the time between starting and finishing the recipe is long, the amount of time spent hovering over the stove really is not very long. The flavors of the meat and the sauce mingle and grow more complex and intense the longer they stay in contact with each other, so do not be afraid to let these short ribs mature in the refrigerator after they have been prepared. Like great Pinot Noir, these ribs evolve into something special with at least a day or two between cooking and serving."

1. In a large bowl combine the ribs, onions, celery, garlic, peppercorns and dried mushrooms. Pour in the wine, mix well, cover and refrigerate overnight.

2. The next day preheat the oven to 250°F. Remove the ribs and pat dry with paper towel. Season the meat well with pepper and salt. Dredge the ribs in flour until lightly coated. Strain the wine marinade into a bowl and reserve the vegetables in a separate bowl.

3. Heat the olive oil over high heat in a large frying pan. Before it burns, place the ribs in the pan and brown on all sides, about 5–7 minutes. You may have to do this in 2 batches. Transfer the ribs to an ovenproof casserole and add the bouquet garni, bay leaves and garlic from the marinade.

4. Remove most of the oil from the frying pan. Add the marinated vegetables, stirring constantly until they begin to brown, 6–7 minutes. Transfer to the casserole with the ribs.

STOLLER VINEYARDS

16161 NE McDougall Road, Dayton
TEL: (503) 864-3404
FAX: (503) 864-2580
www.stollervineyards.com
info@stollervineyards.com

WINE SHOP, TOURS AND TASTINGS
At this stage it's open by appointment
only, but this may change. Check the
website or call for details.

GETTING THERE
Follow Highway 99W from Portland
through Newberg and Dundee. At
Highway 18 (yellow flashing light)
follow McDougall to the west. The
winery driveway is ½ mile down the road.

WINERY HIGHLIGHTS
The winery is one of only two
Oregon wineries to achieve a Gold
LEED Certification (Leadership in
Energy and Environmental Design).
It operates on a gravity-flow design,
has a solar-paneled roof that provides
about 70 percent of the electrical
needs, and uses catacombs to
maintain cool cellar temperatures.

5. Add 2 cups of the reserved wine marinade to the
    frying pan and bring to a boil. Stir until the mixture
    reduces by ¾, about 10–15 minutes. Add another
    2 cups of the marinade, boil and reduce for about
    10 minutes or until the mixture has thickened. Pour
    into the casserole.

6. Mix the tomatoes, stock and remaining reserved wine
    marinade in a frying pan and bring to a boil. Simmer
    for 5 minutes, skim off any grease and transfer to the
    casserole. Cover the casserole and cook for 3–4 hours,
    until the ribs are tender and the meat falls off the
    bone. Remove from the oven.

7. Let the ribs sit in the sauce for at least 1 hour before
    serving. It is even better refrigerated for a day or two.
    Reheat on the stovetop and serve over rice or wide
    egg noodles with Stoller Pinot Noir.

SERVES 6

The Pines 1852 Filet Mignon with Merlot and Mushrooms

featuring THE PINES 1852 MERLOT

6 filet mignon steaks, 1 inch thick (6 oz each)

salt and freshly ground black pepper to taste

3 tsp olive oil

3 Tbsp unsalted butter

2 cloves garlic, minced

1 shallot, diced

1 portobello mushroom, sliced

4 oz crimini mushrooms, sliced

½ cup low sodium beef broth

½ cup Merlot (if you need more wine . . . add more!)

Sierra Wright of The Pines 1852 has developed this elegant recipe that will bring out the best in your filet mignon. These estate-grown 15-year-old vines produce a spicy, full-bodied wine with hints of lush blackberry fruit and black pepper. Enjoy with chocolate, steak, pork and salmon.

1. Season the steaks on both sides with salt and pepper. Heat 2 tsp of the oil and 1 Tbsp of the butter over medium-high heat in a heavy frying pan large enough to fit all of the steaks. Add the steaks and sear both sides until lightly browned, about 2 minutes per side. Remove the steaks to a platter and cover with foil.

2. Preheat the broiler to 500°F. Place the browned steaks on a lightly oiled broiler pan or in an ovenproof frying pan. Broil the steaks on the top rack to the desired doneness, turning them halfway through. Total cooking time is 5 minutes for rare, 7 minutes for medium rare and 9 minutes for medium.

3. As the steaks are cooking, heat the remaining 2 Tbsp butter and 1 tsp oil in the same frying pan used for the steaks. Add the garlic and shallots and sweat for 2–3 minutes. Add the mushrooms and cook until almost done, about 2 minutes. If the pan gets dry, add a bit more butter. Add the beef broth and Merlot. Cook the mixture until it's reduced and slightly thickened, about 2 minutes.

4. Place the steaks on heated plates and spoon the mushroom mixture over each. Enjoy with a glass of The Pines Merlot.

SERVES 6

THE PINES 1852 VINEYARD AND WINERY

5450 Mill Creek Road, The Dalles
TEL: (541) 298-1981
www.thepinesvineyard.com
grapeguyOR@aol.com

WINE SHOP, TOURS AND TASTINGS
Wine tasting and vineyard tours by
appointment only. Contact Sierra
Wright at the number above for more
information.

GETTING THERE
The winery is located off I-84
running along the Columbia River.
Take the The Dalles exit west. Take a
left onto 6th Street. Take a right onto
Cherry Heights. Take a left onto 10th
Street. Take a right onto Mt. Hood.
Mt. Hood turns into Mill Creek. The
driveway is the second left after
Muirhead Cannery.

WINERY HIGHLIGHTS
The winery has one of the oldest
vineyards in the northwest, with Old
Vine Zinfandel plantings dating back
to the late 1800s.

Merlot

pronounced (MARE-LOW)

*Historians have traced Merlot as far back as the first
century in France. Merlot is one of the acclaimed red
varieties of Bordeaux, where it became famous during
the 1800s. This wine is usually a little softer and
perhaps warmer than Cabernet Sauvignon.*

*The wine has been growing in popularity since the late
1970s when winemakers in North America discovered
that the grape is not only good for blending, but also
produces wonderful wine on its own. Its popularity
actually fell a little after the release of the film
Sideways, but we have been assured it's now rising
once again. This is good news as the Pacific Northwest
is recognized as producing some of the best Merlot in
the world.*

*Merlot grapes mature earlier and are larger than the
Cabernet Sauvignon grape. They also have a thicker
skin. This wine is not great for long-term cellaring,
unless it's blended. This probably accounts for some
of its recent popularity, as many consumers prefer the
convenience of having a great wine to drink immediately
rather than waiting for the cellaring process.*

*Common characteristics displayed in Merlot wines
include plum, blackcurrant, cherry, vanilla and cloves.
This wine pairs well with lamb, grilled meats, wild
game, hearty pastas, duck, chocolate and aged cheeses.*

Torii Mor Veal Strudel with Sauce Magritte

featuring TORII MOR PINOT NOIR

3 oz lean smoked bacon, finely diced

1 medium onion, finely diced

2 cloves garlic, minced

1 lb ground veal

1½ cups Pinot Noir

½ lb wild mushrooms

½ shallot, finely diced

2 Tbsp verjus (available at specialty food stores)

3 black peppercorns

4 cups unsalted veal or beef stock (veal is preferred)

½ cup black cherries (fresh or dried)

½ cup fresh raspberries or marionberries

1 Tbsp cornstarch

¼ cup water

3 Tbsp butter

salt to taste

1 package filo pastry, thawed

⅓ cup melted butter

1 Tbsp white sesame seeds

This recipe was created by Richard Gehrts of Red Hills Provincial Dining. The founder of Torii Mor, Donald R. Olsen, instructed the winemaker: "Make me a wine that you can drink with a spoon." From these words have evolved a series of wines that truly express the Oregon terroir.

1. Sauté the bacon to release some fat. Add the onion and garlic and sauté for 2–3 minutes. Add the veal and sauté, stirring to break up any clumps. When it begins to brown, add 1 cup of the Pinot Noir and the mushrooms. Keep stirring until the meat is crumbly and uniformly brown.

2. Drain off the liquid into another pan and reduce until there are only a few tablespoons left. Return the reduced juices to the meat, stir and remove from the heat. Set aside to cool.

3. Simmer the shallot in a saucepan with the remaining ½ cup of Pinot Noir, verjus and peppercorns. Cook until the liquid has almost evaporated. Add the stock and simmer for 15–20 minutes, until it develops a gloss. Add the cherries and berries, cover and simmer for another 15 minutes.

4. Remove from the heat and push the mixture through a strainer. Discard the solids. Mix the cornstarch with the water to make a slurry. Return the sauce to the heat and thicken with the slurry until the sauce coats a spoon. Over a very low heat, use a whisk to beat in the butter. Season with salt.

TORII MOR
440 SE. Maple Street, Dundee
Tasting room:
18325 NE Fairview Drive, Dundee
TEL: 1 (800) 839-5004
FAX: (503) 554-6740
www.toriimorwinery.com
info@toriimorwinery.com

WINE SHOP, TOURS AND TASTINGS
Tasting room open daily 11 a.m.–
5 p.m. Tasting fee $5. Closed Tue.

GETTING THERE
From Portland take I-5 south to 99W.
Follow 99W through to Dundee. In
Dundee turn right onto Ninth Street.
Travel 1 mile and turn right onto NE
Fairview Drive. The tasting room is
on the right.

WINERY HIGHLIGHTS
Sip on some world-class wines in the
ambience of the Japanese gardens.
Enjoy the breathtaking view of Mt.
Hood and the Willamette Valley.

5. Place 1 sheet of filo on a dry work surface and brush with melted butter. Add another sheet and brush again. Repeat until you have 8 sheets stacked, but do not brush the top sheet. Spoon half the meat filling in a line along the bottom edge of the filo. Fold in the sides ½ inch and roll it into a compact cylinder. Seal the edges with butter. Repeat to make 2 rolls.

6. Place the rolls on a cookie sheet seam side down. Brush the outside with melted butter, dust with sesame seeds and bake for about 15 minutes or until golden brown. Allow to sit for 15 minutes. Slice on the bias and serve with the sauce.

SERVES 8

Trium's Butterflied Leg of Lamb with Blue Cheese

featuring TRIUM GROWERS' CUVÉE

1–2 cloves garlic, crushed

1 tsp grated ginger

4 Tbsp brown sugar

½ cup red wine

½ cup soy sauce

½ cup olive oil

1 leg of lamb, butterflied (5 lb)

2 oz blue cheese, crumbled

4 Tbsp butter

4 green onions, chopped

1 Tbsp fresh lemon juice

Growers' Cuvée is a Bordeaux blend of Merlot, Cabernet Sauvignon and Cabernet Franc. This wine has some beautiful cherry and toasted coffee bean flavors with a classic long and elegant finish. It really highlights the lamb, blue cheese and spices in this recipe, which was provided by the winery.

1. In a small bowl combine the garlic, ginger and sugar. Whisk in the wine, soy sauce and olive oil to make the marinade. Place the lamb in a non-reactive container, add the marinade, cover and refrigerate for 2 days. Turn the leg every 4–6 hours.

2. Preheat an outdoor grill to medium-high heat. Combine the cheese, butter, green onions and lemon juice in a bowl. Set aside.

3. Place the lamb on the grill, cover and cook for about 40–60 minutes. A meat thermometer should show an internal temperature of 140°F for medium rare, 150°F for medium and 180°F for well done.

4. Place the lamb on a baking sheet and spoon the blue cheese mixture overtop. Place under the broiler for an additional 4–5 minutes or until the cheese melts and bubbles.

5. To serve, slice thinly. This versatile dish is great with scalloped potatoes, broccoli and baby carrots or, for a more casual dinner, with pitas and fresh salad.

SERVES 6–8

TRIUM WINE
7112 Rapp Lane, Talent
TEL: (541) 535-4015
FAX: (541) 535-6093
www.triumwine.com

WINE SHOP, TOURS AND TASTINGS
Open by appointment only.

GETTING THERE
Take I-5 exit 21 to Highway 99. Go
south on 99 to Rapp Road, about
¾ mile. Follow to Rapp Lane.

WINERY HIGHLIGHTS
There are spectacular views of the
Rogue Valley and winery grounds.

Cabernet Sauvignon

pronounced (CA-BURR-NAY SOH-VIN-YON)

Cabernet Sauvignon, or "Cab Sav" as it is affectionately termed by some wine lovers, is one of the most popular red wines in the world. The grape can be traced back to the Medoc district in the Bordeaux region of France where it is still prominent today.

It's possible that the variety made its first appearance in Oregon as early as the 1880s. The Von Pessls brothers recorded growing the variety "Sauvignon," but it's not known whether this referred to Cabernet or Blanc. So it is generally Richard Sommer of Hillcrest Vineyard who is credited with pioneering Cabernet Sauvignon in Oregon during the late 1960s. The quality of Oregon's Cabernet Sauvignon has skyrocketed over the last decade. The grapes often don't ripen until fairly late in the season and their thick, black skin makes them resistant to frosts.

Cabernet Sauvignon wines are fantastic for aging, and very often good wines will become great wines after cellaring. Cabernet Sauvignon also blends remarkably well and when combined with Merlot it becomes a little mellower without losing its character.

Cabernet Sauvignon pairs superbly with steak, pasta with tomato-based sauces, dark meats, duck, blue cheese and dark chocolate. Known to many as "The King of Red Wine," this variety is unlikely to lose its crown anytime soon.

Kramer's Rabbit with Portobellos and Wild Rice

featuring KRAMER VINEYARDS PINOT NOIR

1 young fryer rabbit, cut in 6 pieces (3–3½ lb)

6 portobello mushrooms, cubed (8 oz each)

1 medium onion, coarsely chopped

4 large cloves garlic, coarsely chopped

poultry seasoning to taste

salt and freshly ground black pepper to taste

1 cup Pinot Noir

3 cups water

3 Tbsp butter

½ cup wild rice

1½ cups brown rice

1 can chicken broth (14 oz)

Created by Marilyn Blen at Kramer Vineyards, this is one of those quick and easy meals that involves throwing some ingredients in a pot and then coming back to enjoy a tasty meal. Judging by the way this tastes, your guests will think you've been slaving away for hours. Kramer Vineyard Pinot Noirs express blackberry, raspberry and plum fruitiness. They're well balanced and elegant, with a medium body and seductive aromatics.

1. Place the meatier pieces of the rabbit on the bottom of a 4-quart saucepan and the smaller pieces on top. Put the mushrooms, onion, garlic, poultry seasoning, salt and pepper over the meat. Pour the wine and 1 cup of the water overtop. Place a tight-fitting lid on the pan and bring to a boil, reduce the heat and simmer for 1 hour.

2. Meanwhile, melt the butter in another saucepan over medium-high heat. Stir in the wild rice and brown it for 3 minutes. Stir in the brown rice. Add the chicken broth and the remaining 2 cups of water and bring to a boil. Reduce the heat and simmer for 30 minutes or until the rice is tender. Turn off the heat and allow the rice to sit for at least 10 minutes before draining off any liquid.

3. Serve the rice with the rabbit, mushrooms and sauce for a simple, but scrumptious meal. Enjoy with a glass of Kramer Pinot Noir.

SERVES 6

KRAMER VINEYARDS

26830 Olson Road, Gaston

TEL: (503) 662-4545

www.kramerwine.com

info@kramerwine.com

WINE SHOP, TOURS AND TASTINGS

Tasting room open daily May–Oct.
and weekends Nov.–Apr., noon–
5 p.m. Closed Jan.–Feb., Christmas
and Easter. Tasting is free unless
you visit during one of their
special events.

GETTING THERE

From Highway 47 in Gaston, turn
west at the Post Office (you can only
turn one way onto Olson Road) and
go 4 miles up Olson Road past Elk
Cove Winery. Just follow the signs,
but be careful on the curves!

WINERY HIGHLIGHTS

Find lovely gifts and tasty treats in
the gift shop. Take advantage of the
large deck with panoramic views
for picnicking. The wedding and
reception site is one of the most
naturally beautiful you will find.
Cassie, the black Labrador featured
on the wine corks, will warmly greet
you and most likely see you to your
car when it's time to go.

Vegetarian

Consuming wine in moderation will help
people to die young as late as possible.

—*Doctor Philip Norrie*

Territorial Cheese Fondue

featuring TERRITORIAL RIESLING

½ lb Gruyère cheese, grated

½ lb Emmenthal cheese, grated

¼ cup all-purpose flour

2 fresh baguettes

1 clove garlic, peeled

2 cups Riesling

1 Tbsp fresh lemon juice

freshly ground black pepper
to taste

There's nothing like sharing a fondue with friends or family to fight off the winter blues. This fondue is made using the Territorial Riesling, which has a secret: nearly 3 percent residual sugar. With an impeccable balance of sugar, acidity, fruit, spice and alcohol, this wine pairs exquisitely with a wide variety of foods and has the crispness of a drier wine.

1. Thoroughly mix the grated cheeses with the flour. Cut the bread into bite-sized cubes and bake in the oven on cookie sheets at a low heat until warm and slightly toasted.

2. Rub the inside of a small flame-proof casserole dish with the garlic clove. Add the wine and lemon juice. Heat over high heat until near boiling. Add the cheese mixture, 1 handful at a time, stirring constantly. Season with pepper to taste.

3. Transfer to a fondue pot or set the dish on a warming device in the middle of the table. Accompany with bread cubes or your favorite vegetables. For a truly hands-on dinner, serve whole cooked artichokes.

SERVES 4

TERRITORIAL VINEYARDS & WINE COMPANY

907 West 3rd Avenue, Eugene
TEL: (541) 684-9463
FAX: (541) 434-8463
www.territorialvineyards.com
alan@territorialvineyards.com

WINE SHOP, TOURS AND TASTINGS
Open Fri.–Sat. 2 p.m.–7 p.m. and Thu.
5 p.m.–11 p.m. with live music!

GETTING THERE
Located in downtown Eugene. From
I-5 take exit 194B to Eugene,
following the signs to Florence. This
runs onto Sixth Avenue. Turn right
on Adams and travel 3 blocks to the
corner of Adams and 3rd.

WINERY HIGHLIGHTS
Wine Press Northwest magazine voted
Territorial Vineyards "2005 Oregon
Winery of the Year to Watch." All
fruit comes from estate-owned
and/or estate-managed vineyards.

Spaghetti Mediterranean

featuring SEMILLON

1½ lb spaghetti

¼ cup olive oil

5 cloves garlic, crushed

1 onion, finely chopped

¼ cup Semillon

6 ripe tomatoes, chopped

¾ cup black olives, pitted

¼ cup capers

½ cup chopped fresh basil

1 cup crumbled feta cheese

salt and freshly ground black
    pepper to taste

basil sprigs for garnish

If you use fresh ingredients this may well become your favorite pasta dish. We suggest you buy the black olives with pits in and remove them yourself as their flavor is superior. Feta is commonly used throughout the Mediterranean and the 14th-century Venetian cookbook Libro per Cuoco *contains two recipes that use feta.*

1. Cook the spaghetti until *al dente* in a large pot of salted water. (See the package for exact directions, usually about 8 minutes.) Drain and set aside.

2. Heat the olive oil in a large sauté pan over medium heat and sauté the garlic for 1 minute. Add the onion and sauté for 2 minutes. Add the wine, tomatoes, olives, capers and basil and sauté for 3–4 minutes. Finally, add the feta and drained spaghetti and toss well in the pan to combine.

3. When everything is hot, divide the pasta among individual bowls and garnish with additional sprigs of basil.

SERVES 6

Semillon

Pronounced (SEH-MEE-YON)

Semillon is best known for being blended with Sauvignon Blanc to create the dry white wines of Bordeaux. It's also commonly blended with Chardonnay, but it's an outstanding wine on its own. As well as being a table wine, it is used to make dessert wines when affected by **Botrytis cinerea**, *also called noble rot.*

Semillon does well all over the world, and countries as diverse as Israel, Portugal, Tunisia, Australia, Argentina and South Africa produce great wines from this grape. It's believed that at one time Semillon was the world's most commonly grown grape.

It's widely planted in southern Oregon, especially around the Rouge River Valley. It ripens earlier than many other varieties, which makes it less susceptible to frosts. The grapes are thick-skinned and are generally a dark shade of yellow, although sometimes they gain a slight pink tinge.

Semillon, like Riesling, develops very well in the bottle and can be cellared for 5 years with excellent results. After aging, hazelnut characteristics are common. When consumed young, the wine has a figgy, sometimes floral flavor. This wine pairs very well with risotto, pilaf and other grain dishes, as well as fish and seafood.

Erath Vineyards Braised Sugar Pumpkin with Black Pepper Spaetzle

featuring ERATH PINOT NOIR ESTATE SELECTION

1 bottle Pinot Noir

¼ cup Saba dressing or balsamic vinegar

1 cinnamon stick

2 cloves

2 allspice berries

1 tsp grated orange zest

8 peppercorns

1 medium sugar pumpkin, cut into 6 wedges

½ cup milk

1 egg, beaten

1 cup all-purpose flour

2 Tbsp minced fresh herbs, such as thyme, parsley and chives

1 tsp salt

1 Tbsp freshly ground black pepper

1 Tbsp olive oil

2 Tbsp butter

salt and freshly ground black pepper to taste

Chef Adam Sappington of the Wildwood restaurant in Portland created this fabulous recipe for Erath. Erath grows Pinot Noir at six different sites in the Dundee Hills viticultural area. "Reserve" quality lots are chosen from the best wines made from these sites and these are blended to make this Estate Selection cuveé. Fruit-focused in their youth, the Estate Selection Pinots gain additional complexity and sophistication when cellared for three to eight years.

1. Preheat the oven to 325°F. Combine the wine, vinegar, cinnamon, cloves, allspice, orange zest and peppercorns in a saucepan and bring to a boil. Reduce the heat and allow to simmer for a minute.

2. Place the pumpkin wedges in a shallow baking dish. Pour the simmering mixture over the pumpkin, cover and bake for 45 minutes or until there is no resistance when the pumpkin is pierced with a knife. Remove the pumpkin, cover and set aside.

3. Whisk together the milk and egg in a bowl. Whisk in the flour until smooth and add the herbs, salt and pepper.

ERATH VINEYARDS
9409 NE Worden Hill Road, Dundee
TEL: (503) 538-3318
FAX: (503) 538-1074
www.erath.com
info@erath.com

WINE SHOP, TOURS AND TASTINGS
Tasting room open 11 a.m.–5 p.m.
daily, except major holidays. Tours
of the cellar and VIP tastings are
available by appointment only, based
on availability, with a maximum
capacity for 40 people per tour.

GETTING THERE
From Portland take 99W west
through Newberg to Dundee. In
Dundee, turn right on Ninth Street
and follow it through until it turns
into Worden Hill Road.

WINERY HIGHLIGHTS
During the annual chef series "Wine
Country Cooking in the Dundee Hills,"
celebrated chefs from around the
globe fly in and cook up tantalizing
cuisine to pair with Erath wines.

4. Bring a large pot of water to a rolling boil. Place
a large colander or perforated pan over, but not
touching, the boiling water. Pour the batter into the
colander or pan. Use a rubber spatula to quickly press
the batter through the holes into the boiling water.
Once all of the batter has been forced through the
holes, remove the colander or pan. Stir the spaetzle
and cook for 1 minute. Drain well. Toss with the olive
oil and set aside.

5. Using a 10-inch non-stick frying pan, melt the butter
over medium-high heat. Add the spaetzle and season
with salt and pepper. Cook until brown and crispy.
Serve with the pumpkin and Erath Pinot Noir.

SERVES 2–4

Spanakopita

2 packages frozen spinach
(10 oz each)

2 Tbsp olive oil

3 cloves garlic, crushed

1 cup chopped onion

½ cup white wine

4 oz feta cheese

1 tub ricotta (8 oz)

salt and freshly ground black
pepper to taste

12 sheets filo pastry

½ cup melted butter

Historians have recently discovered what may be the remains of a spanakopita feast in the tomb of the legendary King Midas of Macedonia. Today this traditional Greek snack is popular the world over. Some people are nervous about cooking with filo pastry, but it's much easier than you think and even a novice cook can re-create the "Midas touch" for this delicious dish.

1. Preheat the oven to 350°F. Thaw the spinach according to the directions on the package and drain well.

2. Heat the olive oil in a pan over medium heat. Add the garlic and onion and sauté for 3 minutes. Add the spinach and wine and stir well. Sauté for 2–3 minutes before transferring the spinach mixture to a large bowl. Set aside for a few minutes to cool. Add the feta and ricotta and use your hands (be careful, the spinach is hot) to mix thoroughly. Season with salt and pepper.

3. Lay 1 sheet of filo pastry on a work surface (with the long side of the rectangle facing you), and brush it with the melted butter. Stack another sheet on top and brush it with butter. Repeat with a third sheet and then a fourth, but do not butter the fourth. Using a sharp knife, cut the pastry into 3 equal-sized rectangles. The short side of each rectangle should now be facing you.

4. Drop ¹⁄₁₂ of the spinach mixture in the bottom right corner of each filo rectangle about 1 inch from the end. Form a triangle by folding one corner over the filling. Continue to fold the strip up and over, ending with a triangle shape. Brush each triangle with butter and place on a baking tray. You now have 3 triangles; repeat the filo pastry process until you have 12.

5. Bake for 20–25 minutes or until the pastry is golden brown and crispy. Serve 2 triangles per person.

SERVES 6

Gourmet Baked Macaroni & Cheese

For years—in fact, centuries—macaroni and cheese has been considered one of the world's great comfort foods. Thomas Jefferson is reported to have served macaroni and cheese at the White House in 1802. The dish became even more poplar when Kraft released their version in 1937. This version includes some tomatoes and some wine to give it the gourmet cachet.

1. Preheat the oven to 350°F. Heat the oil in a large pan over medium heat. Add the onion and sauté for about 3 minutes, stirring frequently. Add the garlic and lightly season with salt and pepper. Continue to sauté for another 2 minutes.

2. Add the tomatoes and increase the heat to high. Cook, stirring frequently, for about 15 minutes, until the liquid has evaporated. Reduce the heat to medium-high, then add the wine, basil, oregano and sugar. Cook for about 10 minutes, until the liquid is nearly gone.

3. Remove the pan from the heat. Add the cooked macaroni and 1 cup of the cheddar cheese. Mix well. Put the macaroni mixture in a greased ovenproof dish and cover with the remaining cheddar and the Parmesan cheese. Bake for 40–45 minutes or until the cheese is golden brown and bubbling. Serve immediately.

SERVES 4–6

1 Tbsp olive oil

½ onion, diced

3 cloves garlic, crushed

salt and freshly ground black pepper to taste

1 can chopped tomatoes (28 oz)

⅔ cup red wine

3 Tbsp chopped fresh basil

1 Tbsp chopped fresh oregano

1½ tsp sugar

5 cups macaroni cooked *al dente* (about 2½ cups uncooked macaroni)

2 cups grated aged cheddar cheese

½ cup grated Parmesan cheese

Seufort Winery Jeweled Couscous

featuring SEUFERT WINERY WOVEN WHITE

2 cups dry couscous

1 cup pine nuts

1 Tbsp olive oil

¼ cup finely diced red onion

2 Tbsp finely chopped shallot

1 cup white wine

2 cups orange juice (preferably freshly squeezed)

½ cup finely diced dried apricots

¼ cup white raisins, finely diced

½ cup dried cranberries, finely diced

½ preserved lemon with juice, finely diced rind and flesh (optional—see chef's tip next page)

1 tsp each ground allspice, ground coriander and ground turmeric

½ tsp each ground cumin, cinnamon, nutmeg, cardamom and ginger

¼ tsp ground cloves

¼ cup fresh pomegranate seeds

Winemaker Jim Seufert created this vegetarian dish that transforms the classic Middle Eastern staple. The jewel-like fruits add color and fresh, intense flavors that complement the traditional spice blend. Seufert Winery Woven White is a light-bodied, slightly acidic wine designed to pair well with a wide variety of foods.

1. Prepare the couscous according to package instructions. Set aside in a large bowl. Heat a frying pan over medium heat and lightly toast the pine nuts, being careful not to burn them. Set aside.

2. Heat the olive oil over medium heat and sauté the onion and shallot until soft, 5–6 minutes. Add the wine and orange juice. When the liquid is hot, add the apricots, raisins, cranberries and preserved lemon (if using). Add all the spices and stir to blend thoroughly. Simmer, stirring occasionally, until the liquid thickens and reduces by at least half, about 25–30 minutes. Remove from the heat.

3. Add the toasted pine nuts to the couscous. Pour the sauce and fruit mixture over the couscous and mix gently to blend. Sprinkle the pomegranate seeds overtop. Enjoy hot or chilled.

SERVES 6–8

SEUFERT WINERY

22734 SW Latham Road, McMinnville

TEL: (503) 709-1255

www.seufertwinery.com

jim@seufertwinery.com

WINE SHOP, TOURS AND TASTINGS
Tastings and winery tours by
appointment only.

GETTING THERE
From McMinnville, follow Highway 18
west for 8 miles. Turn right onto Muddy
Valley Road, left onto Latham Road
and right onto Redhawk Road. Seufert
Winery shares facilities with Coleman
Vineyard—look for their signs.

WINERY HIGHLIGHTS
Limited volume allows winemaker Jim
Seufert, a fourth-generation Oregonian,
to focus on wine quality, resulting in
what he calls "wine with soul."

WINERY SPECIAL OFFER
If you show your copy of this book, two
people can taste for the price of one.

CHEF'S TIP

*The recipe can be successfully made without the
preserved lemons, but they do add an authentic
Mediterranean flavor. To preserve lemons, clean
2 lemons and cut each into 8 wedges. In a small sealed
glass jar mix the wedges with ⅓ cup coarse sea salt. Add
½ cup fresh lemon juice and store at room temperature
for 1 week, shaking daily to distribute the juice and
salt. Use immediately or store in the fridge for up to
1 week. They are especially good tossed in a green salad.*

Side Dishes

I think it is a great error to consider a tax
on wines as a tax on luxury. On the contrary
it is a tax on the health of our citizens.

—Thomas Jefferson

Grilled Asparagus with Cheese Fonduta and Toasted Hazelnuts

featuring PINOT GRIS

2 lb local asparagus, woody ends cut off

6 cups whipping cream

4 oz soft goat cheese at room temperature

1 Tbsp Pinot Gris (Chef Turke used champagne vinegar)

½ cup Oregon hazelnuts, skins removed and roughly chopped

¼ cup extra virgin olive oil

salt and freshly ground black pepper to taste

This delightful recipe is adapted from one provided by Chef Christopher Turke of the Tuscany Grill in Portland. It's included here as a side, but it also makes a great appetizer. The sauce is the key to this pairing, as the nuttiness, creaminess and subtle acids from the cheese are matched with the same nuances in the Pinot Gris. This dish was created using the Cooper Mountain "Reserve" Pinot Gris.

1. Bring a large pot of salted water to a boil. Prepare a bowl with ice and water. Drop the asparagus into the boiling water for 2 minutes. Transfer immediately to the ice bath to stop the asparagus from cooking. When completely chilled, remove the asparagus from the water and set aside.

2. In a heavy saucepan over medium heat reduce the cream by half. Do this slowly or the cream will spill over. (Chef Turke claims that putting a silver spoon in the saucepan will keep the cream from bubbling over.) Toss in the goat cheese, wine and a pinch of salt.

3. Remove from the heat and use a hand blender or whisk to blend in the cheese. Adjust the seasoning with salt and pepper and let the sauce cool at room temperature.

4. Preheat the grill to high. Toast the hazelnuts in a dry sauté pan on the grill or on a stovetop until lightly colored and fragrant, 2–3 minutes. Crush the toasted nuts. Toss the asparagus in the olive oil and season with salt and pepper. Grill for 5–7 minutes or until slightly charred.

5. Pool the sauce on the plate, add the asparagus and sprinkle the hazelnuts overtop.

SERVES 6–8

Baked Tomatoes with Parmesan Cheese

These juicy wine-doused tomatoes are an excellent addition to almost any meal. The best thing about this dish is that it brings out so many flavors from the tomatoes. The hot tomato juice mixed with the wine is just divine.

4 large tomatoes

salt and freshly ground black pepper to taste

3 Tbsp olive oil

2 cloves garlic, crushed

¼ cup finely chopped basil

½ cup white wine

4 Tbsp grated Parmesan cheese

1. Preheat the oven to 350°F. Cut the bottom off each tomato so it sits flat. Slice the tomatoes in half horizontally and place them in a small non-metallic baking dish with the centers facing up. Sprinkle with salt and pepper.

2. Combine the oil, garlic and basil in a small bowl and mix well. Place the mixture on top of the tomatoes, trying to keep as much on the tomatoes as possible. Pour the wine into the pan around (not on) the tomatoes.

3. Sprinkle the tomatoes with the cheese and bake for 40 minutes.

4. Serve with some of the wine sauce poured overtop.

SERVES 4

Butternut Squash & Hazelnut Risotto

featuring PINOT BLANC

⅓ cup hazelnuts, chopped

4 cups vegetable broth

2 Tbsp olive oil

2½ cups peeled butternut squash, cubed

3 cloves garlic, minced

¼ cup finely chopped onion

½ cup finely chopped celery

1 cup chopped mushrooms (use wild mushrooms if you can get them)

1½ cups arborio rice

½ tsp ground nutmeg

1 cup white wine

kosher salt and freshly ground black pepper to taste

¼ cup butter, cubed

3 tsp finely chopped fresh thyme

½ cup grated Parmesan cheese

We love recipes with exciting textures, and the crisp toasted hazelnuts contrast beautifully with the creamy risotto. Oregon is responsible for around 99 percent of all hazelnut production in the United States. Hazelnuts are very high in dietary fiber, iron, potassium, vitamin E, calcium and magnesium—and they taste great too!

1. Toast the hazelnuts in a dry frying pan over medium heat until they are warm, aromatic and slightly browned. Set aside.

2. Bring the broth to a simmer in a medium saucepan.

3. Heat the olive oil in a large saucepan over medium-high heat. Add the squash and sauté for 4–5 minutes until soft. Add the garlic, onion and celery and stir for 2 minutes before adding the mushrooms. Stir for a further 2 minutes, then add the rice and nutmeg and stir for 1–2 minutes. Add the wine and continue stirring until the wine has been absorbed.

4. Add ½ cup of the simmering vegetable broth to the rice. Reduce the heat and simmer, stirring constantly, until the liquid is almost absorbed, about 3 minutes. Continue adding broth, stirring after each addition until the liquid is absorbed, until it has all been used or the rice has reached your desired texture. The rice should be creamy but firm in the center. Season with salt and pepper.

5. Remove from the heat and stir in the butter, thyme and cheese. Serve in individual bowls and top each with the toasted hazelnuts.

SERVES 4

Looking through a glass of wine is a great way to examine the spectacular Erath Vineyards (page 135)

PREVIOUS PAGE: Scott Paul Braised Chicken with Morels (page 90)

The incredible view from Anne Amie Vineyards (page 149) PHOTO COURTESY OF ANNE AMIE

Everyone gets called in to help pick the grapes at Paradis Vineyard (page 175)

OPPOSITE: Airlie Winery's Incredible Foch Lamb Shanks (page 96)

Ponzi's Aurora Vineyard, first planted in 1991 atop Chehalem Mountain, is the perfect location
to grow Pinot Noir and Pinot Gris (page 185) JOHN MCANULTY PHOTO
OPPOSITE: Cherry Hill's Venison Medallions with Sun-Dried Berry Demi-Glace (page 104)
NEXT PAGE: Ribbon Ridge Vineyards Chocolate Lavender Torte with Muscat Sabayon (page 186)

Broccoli and Cauliflower Baked in Cheesy Wine Sauce

Serve this simple, tasty dish as a side or make a meal by using it as the topping for baked potatoes. You can substitute broccoflowers, a cross between broccoli and cauliflower, which looks like a green cauliflower with a texture more like broccoli.

1. Preheat the oven to 375°F. Bring a large pot of salted water to a boil. Add the cauliflower and cook for about 2 minutes before adding the broccoli. Cook together for about 5 minutes, until just tender. Drain and transfer to a deep ovenproof dish.

2. Melt the butter in a saucepan over medium heat. Add the shallots and garlic, sautéing for 1 minute. Add the flour and stir well for about 1 minute. Reduce the heat to medium-low. Gradually add the wine, stirring continuously. Add the cream, ⅓ cup of the cheese, paprika and dried mustard. Continue stirring until the cheese has melted and you have a thick creamy sauce. Season with salt and pepper.

3. Pour the sauce evenly over the broccoli and cauliflower mixture, sprinkle with the remaining cheese and bake for 25–30 minutes, until the cheese is golden brown and bubbling. Serve immediately.

SERVES 4–6

½ lb cauliflower

1 lb broccoli florets

2 Tbsp butter

⅓ cup finely chopped shallots

1 clove garlic, crushed

2 Tbsp all-purpose flour

1 cup white wine

½ cup whipping cream

⅔ cup grated aged cheddar cheese

1 tsp paprika

½ tsp dried mustard

salt and freshly ground black pepper to taste

Tender Baby Potatoes in Wine

1½ lb baby potatoes

2 cups white wine

2 Tbsp butter

2 cloves garlic, crushed

1 tsp salt

¼ cup chopped fresh chives

Use any variety of potato you like—red, white or purple. There aren't many recipes where potatoes are cooked in wine, which is surprising because the results are fantastic. Try it for yourself in this easy-to-make side dish.

1. Scrub unpeeled potatoes and place in a medium-sized pan. Add the wine, butter, garlic and salt. Cover and bring to a boil over high heat. Reduce the heat to medium-low and simmer for about 10–12 minutes, until the potatoes are just tender.

2. Remove the potatoes with a slotted spoon and keep warm.

3. Increase the temperature to high and reduce the liquid to about ⅔ cup.

4. Serve the potatoes with the wine sauce and sprinkle with chives.

SERVES 4–6

Garlic Mushrooms

Fresh mushrooms and wine, especially Chardonnay, are made for each other. This makes a great side dish, but it's also a fabulous stuffing for a breakfast or brunch omelet.

¼ cup olive oil

1 lb small whole button mushrooms

2 Tbsp butter

3 cloves garlic, crushed

salt to taste

½ cup white wine

1 Tbsp chopped fresh parsley

1. Heat the oil in a large frying pan over high heat. Add the mushrooms. Let the bottoms brown before stirring occasionally. Sauté for about 5 minutes, until well browned on all sides.

2. Reduce the heat a little and add the butter, stirring it through the mushrooms. When the butter has completely melted, add the garlic and salt. Sauté for another 3 minutes, then add the wine. Cook until most of the liquid has evaporated.

3. Stir in the parsley and serve immediately.

SERVES 4–6

Risotto Anne Amie

featuring ANNE AMIE PINOT NOIR

½ cup unsalted butter

1 small onion, finely chopped

2 cups Italian arborio or carnaroli rice (you cannot substitute regular rice!)

1 cup Pinot Noir

10 cups hot broth

½ oz dried porcini mushrooms, rehydrated in warm water for 2 hours, chopped (liquid reserved)

salt to taste

½ cup grated Parmigiano Reggiano cheese

Risotto can be the most wonderful of dishes when done right. When done wrong, it's just mush. Here are some tips to make sure your risotto is perfect. First, the better your broth, the better the risotto! It's better to use homemade broth than commercial stock as the stock has flavors that can be too intense: an easy method for homemade broth is to simmer a piece of meat and bones with some vegetables for a few hours. Second, it's important that the broth is very hot when added. Third, there are no shortcuts to a great risotto. The rice will need your full attention for at least 20 minutes.

1. In a large, heavy sauté pan, melt all but 2 Tbsp of the butter over medium heat. Do not let the butter brown. Add the onion and lightly sauté until just translucent. Do not let it brown. From now on you will have to continue stirring until the risotto is finished!

2. Once the onion is cooked, add the rice and toss well with the butter and onion to coat each grain. Increase the heat to medium-high and toss for 1 minute. Add the wine and cook until it's absorbed. Add the chopped mushrooms and a ladle of the hot water that was used to hydrate them. When it's absorbed start adding the hot broth, a ladle at a time. Cook and stir until it's almost absorbed before adding the next ladle.

ANNE AMIE VINEYARDS
6580 NE Mineral Springs Road
Carlton
TEL: (503) 864-2991
FAX: (503) 864-2203
www.anneamie.com
contactus@anneamie.com

WINE SHOP, TOURS AND TASTINGS
Tasting room open daily 10 a.m.–
5 p.m. Tasting fee of $5 and
reservations are required for groups
of 8 or more.

GETTING THERE
Head south from Portland on I-5,
take the Tiggard-99W exit 294 and
continue south on 99W through to
Layfette. Go through Layfette and
take the first right as you come out
of town, Mineral Springs Road. Anne
Amie is 1½ miles down the road.

WINERY HIGHLIGHTS
The winery is reminiscent of the
French countryside, with breathtaking
views of the estate vineyard and the
Pacific Coast Range.

3. Start tasting the rice after 15 minutes to check the cooking progress. Each grain should have a little resistance but should not be crunchy. Season with salt, keeping in mind that the cheese also adds a salty flavor. The risotto should be quite moist. It will look and taste creamy.

4. When the rice is just short of being done, remove from the heat and stir in the remaining butter and the cheese. Serve immediately with additional freshly grated Parmigiano Reggiano and a bottle of Anne Amie Pinot Noir.

SERVES 4

Sauces & Marinades

Good wine ruins the purse,
bad wine ruins the stomach.

—Spanish proverb

Abacela Spanish Meatball Sauce

featuring Abacela Tempranillo

1 cup Tempranillo

1 Tbsp liquid browning sauce
(or liquid smoke)

1 can tomato paste (4 oz)

½ cup brown sugar

2 Tbsp finely chopped fresh
sage

1 Tbsp red chili powder

1 Tbsp ground white pepper

4 cans beef broth (12 oz each)

1 can crushed or finely diced
tomatoes (12 oz)

½ cup butter

2 Tbsp all-purpose flour

salt to taste

1½–3 tsp cayenne powder

2½ lb cooked meatballs

This is a simple feast dish that's easily doubled for a larger gathering. The Abacela Tempranillo has the typical varietal characteristics of ripe blackberry and plum. Mineral, cedar and tobacco persist from the bold entry through to the lengthy finish. It's a good match for this meatball sauce.

1. Boil the wine in a large, deep saucepan over high heat until it reduces by half. Add the browning sauce, tomato paste, brown sugar, sage, chili powder and white pepper.

2. Reduce the heat to medium and simmer for 5 minutes. Add the beef broth, tomatoes with their juice and at least 2 cups of water. Cook over medium heat for 30 minutes.

3. Soften the butter in the microwave or in a saucepan. Whisk in just enough flour to make a slightly stiff but pliable consistency. Blend thoroughly into the sauce and simmer over low heat for 15 minutes.

4. Add the salt, cayenne pepper and meatballs and simmer over low heat for 20–30 minutes.

5. Serve over your choice of pasta and enjoy with a glass of Abacela Tempranillo.

Serves 6–8

ABACELA VINEYARDS AND
WINERY
12500 Lookingglass Road, Roseburg
TEL: (541) 679-6642
FAX: (541) 679-4455
www.abacela.com
wine@abacela.com

WINE SHOP, TOURS AND TASTINGS
Tasting room open daily 11 a.m.–5 p.m.

GETTING THERE
Traveling southbound on I-5, take
exit 119. Follow US 99/42 to the third
stoplight. Turn right onto US 42 west.
Turn right at the caution light at
Brockway Road. Go north for about
1 mile then turn left onto Lookingglass
Road. After ½ mile turn right into the
gated driveway.

WINERY HIGHLIGHTS
The vineyards are planted on fault
lines with vast differences in the soils
on either side. Ask about how this
affects the qualities of the grapes
grown here.

Tempranillo

pronounced (TEMP-RAH-NEE-YO)

*This famous Spanish grape is the key to the excellent
Rioja wines you may have tried. It is often touted as
"the Spanish version of Cabernet Sauvignon." The grape
is also called "Cencibel" and "Valdepeñas."*

*In Oregon, the wine is produced by several wineries,
with some excellent examples coming from Abacela
Vineyards in the Umpqua Valley, where the vines were
first planted in 1995. Keep an eye on this varietal; we
predict it will soon experience a huge boom throughout
the Pacific Northwest.*

*The grape is thick skinned and very dark in color. Its
name comes from the Spanish word* **temprano** *meaning
"early" and it does ripen earlier than the other Spanish
varietals.*

*The wine is usually medium to full bodied and is
fantastic for aging. Common characteristics include
flavors of vanilla, cedar and spice with aromas of ripe
berries, plum, leather, spice and cassis. Tempranillo is
excellent with Spanish tapas and pairs well with lamb,
ham and most vegetables.*

Teriyaki Marinade

¾ cup red wine
2 Tbsp olive oil
1½ cups soy sauce
1 clove garlic, crushed
½ cup brown sugar
1 tsp sesame oil
1 piece grated ginger (1 inch)

This adaptation of a traditional Japanese recipe uses wine to make the meat even more flavorsome than usual. Marinated meat can be pan-fried or cooked on the barbecue. Try this with kebabs, steaks, chicken, salmon and even prawns.

1. Combine all the ingredients and marinate the meat. Beef should be marinated overnight, chicken 2–3 hours and fish for about 30 minutes.

MAKES 2½–3 CUPS

Spicy Marinade for Beef

¼ cup red wine
½ cup vegetable oil
1 tsp cayenne pepper
2 cloves garlic, crushed
¼ cup balsamic vinegar
2 tsp dried thyme

This simple marinade works especially well with kebabs. Thread some cubes of marinated steak on skewers with your favorite vegetables and turn up at a local barbecue and you'll definitely be invited back.

1. Combine all the ingredients with the meat and refrigerate overnight in a sealed container. Beef should be marinated for at least 5 hours and up to 24 hours. Turn occasionally.

MAKES 1 CUP

Perfect Pasta Sauce

Sometimes all you want is a recipe that tastes great and is easy to prepare. This is it! There are no exotic ingredients here, but when these common ingredients are combined in the right proportions something magical happens. It's a recipe you'll want to keep close at hand.

2 Tbsp butter

2 Tbsp olive oil

2 cups sliced fresh button mushrooms

3 cloves garlic, crushed

½ cup white wine

1 can chopped tomatoes (28 oz)

½ cup whipping cream

salt and freshly ground black pepper to taste

chopped parsley for garnish

1. Melt the butter with the olive oil in a frying pan over medium-high heat. Add the mushrooms and sauté until they begin to soften, 4–5 minutes. Add the garlic and cook for another 2–3 minutes.

2. Add the wine and canned tomatoes with their juice. Bring to a boil, then reduce the heat and simmer for 2–3 minutes before adding the cream. Stir and season with salt and pepper.

3. Serve over hot pasta that has been tossed with Parmesan cheese. Garnish liberally with chopped parsley.

SERVES 4

Rosemary Marinade for Steak in Minutes

¼ cup red wine

1 Tbsp Worcestershire sauce

1 Tbsp balsamic vinegar

2 Tbsp chopped fresh
rosemary

2 cloves garlic, crushed

1 Tbsp Dijon mustard

2 Tbsp tomato paste

If you're pressed for time and want a marinade that will work wonders in only minutes, look no further. Marinate a steak for just 20 minutes and it will make a world of difference. Marinate it for an hour and it will be sublime. This is also great on chicken, pork or lamb.

1. This is as easy as combining the ingredients and marinating the meat.

2. Resealable plastic bags are easy to use: they seal in the flavor and keep the air out.

MAKES 1 CUP

Creamy White/Cheese Sauce

This versatile sauce enhances fish, poultry and gratin dishes and can be used as base for many other sauces. If the milk is hot when you add it to the flour and butter mixture, there should be no lumps. But if lumps do form, just process the sauce in a blender for a few seconds.

1½ cups milk
4 Tbsp butter
3 Tbsp all-purpose flour
½ cup white wine
salt to taste
dash cayenne pepper
¾ cup grated cheese (optional)

1. Bring the milk to a simmer in a small saucepan.

2. In a separate saucepan melt the butter over medium heat. Add the flour, stirring until combined.

3. Slowly add the hot milk to the flour/butter mixture, stirring constantly until the sauce thickens. Add the white wine and continue to simmer and stir over very low heat for about 10 minutes. Season with salt and cayenne pepper. If you are making a white sauce, you're finished at this point.

4. For cheese sauce, add the grated cheese and stir well. Remove from the heat when all the cheese has melted into the sauce.

MAKES 2 CUPS

Coelho Winery of Amity Raspberry Thyme Sauce

featuring RENOVAÇÃO PINOT GRIS

1 tsp grapeseed oil

fresh crushed hot peppers to taste (chipotle are also very good)

⅓ cup raspberry jam

1 cup Pinot Gris

1 tsp chopped fresh thyme

This incredibly versatile sauce can be served on anything from cheesecake to New York steak. An aroma of pear can be caught drifting up from the glass the moment this fresh, crisp Pinot Gris is poured. The fruit is balanced nicely, with a hint of green grass on the palate.

1. Put the grapeseed oil in a small non-reactive saucepan over medium heat. Add the hot peppers and brown evenly, about 4 minutes. Add the raspberry jam and stir until caramelized, about 4–5 minutes.

2. Add the Pinot Gris, reserving 1 tsp of the wine for later use. Bring to a boil. Reduce the heat and simmer for about 30 minutes, until the wine reduces to the consistency of hot syrup. Stir often.

3. Add the thyme, mix well and remove from the heat. Let the sauce stand for a couple of minutes.

4. Strain while hot and add the reserved 1 tsp of Pinot Gris, mixing it in well. The sauce can be served hot or cold.

MAKES ½ CUP

COELHO WINERY OF AMITY
111 5th Street, Amity
TEL: (503) 835-9305
FAX: (503) 835-5041
www.coelhowinery.com
coelhowinery@onlinemac.com

WINE SHOP, TOURS AND TASTINGS
Open Jun.-Nov., Fri.-Sun. 11 a.m.-
5 p.m. From Dec.-May open the
first weekend of every month.
Tasting fee of $5 includes a taste
of Renovação Pinot Gris, Theia
Chardonnay, Paciencia Pinot Noir
and Hyperion Syrah.

GETTING THERE
Follow Highway 99W south of
McMinnville to Amity. Turn west on
Fifth Street (Bellview Highway) and
Coelho Winery is on the left before
the railroad tracks.

WINERY HIGHLIGHTS
An historic building built in the
1930s was renovated using the huge
wooden beams of the original. There
is a cozy fireplace and plenty of
seating to relax and enjoy a glass of
wine. This area is available for events
of up to 100 people.

WINERY SPECIAL OFFER
If you show this book you'll receive
a free souvenir wine glass with your
tasting.

The Essence of Yamhill Valley Vineyard Pinot Noir

featuring YAMHILL VALLEY VINEYARD PINOT NOIR

7 Tbsp butter

1 lb onions, chopped

3 cups Pinot Noir

3 cups unsalted beef stock

The sweet, dark fruit character, tannins and acids of the wine make this a fantastic sauce for beef, pork or chicken. Use it for elegant weekend entertaining or just to spark up a weeknight meal.

1. Melt 4 Tbsp of butter in a large deep pan over medium heat and sauté the onions until softened, around 5 minutes. Transfer to a food processor or blender and purée until smooth. Return to the pan.

2. Add the wine and simmer until the mixture has reduced by half. Add the beef stock and continue to simmer until the mixture has reduced by half again.

3. Whisk in the remaining 3 Tbsp butter and serve immediately. The sauce can be stored in the refrigerator for 3–4 days. Just heat before serving.

MAKES A LITTLE OVER 2½ CUPS

YAMHILL VALLEY VINEYARDS

16250 SW Oldsville Road,
McMinnville
TEL: (503) 843-3100
FAX: (503) 843-2450
www.yamhill.com
info@yamhill.com

WINE SHOP, TOURS AND TASTINGS
Open daily 11 a.m.–5 p.m. from
Memorial Day through to
Thanksgiving weekend. Open
mid–Mar. to Memorial Day, Sat.–
Sun. 11 a.m.–5 p.m. Closed during
the winter months except the first
three weekends of Dec. There is no
tasting fee.

GETTING THERE
The vineyard is 4 miles west of
McMinnville on Highway 18.

WINERY HIGHLIGHTS
Try the exceptional wines from the
Pinot family: Noir, Blanc and Gris.
Make use of the large deck for a
picnic. Check out the koi pond and
feed the fish.

Citrus Wine Marinade

¼ cup olive oil

2 Tbsp fresh lemon juice

2 Tbsp lime juice

2 Tbsp brown sugar

¼ cup white wine

1 Tbsp fresh thyme

2 cloves garlic, minced

2 tsp grated lemon rind

This is perfect for fish and chicken on the grill. The lime and lemon juice give it some zing and the wine and thyme add depth of flavor.

1. Just mix all the ingredients together in a non-reactive container.

2. Chicken should marinate about 3 hours and fish for 30 minutes.

MAKES 1 CUP

Honey Mustard Marinade

This version of the popular honey mustard marinade features white wine and is a big hit with chicken or pork, but it also goes well with salmon. Make sure you reduce the marinating time for fish as it can become mushy if it marinates longer than 30 minutes. You can baste the fish with leftover marinade as you're cooking.

1 cup white wine
½ cup Dijon mustard
¾ cup olive oil
¼ cup honey
2 cloves garlic, crushed
2 Tbsp soy sauce

1. Combine all the marinade ingredients in a bowl.

2. Place the marinade and meat or fish in a sealed non-reactive container. Refrigerate at least 3 hours for pork or chicken and 30 minutes for fish.

Makes 2½ cups

Dominio IV Syrah Coffee Reduction

featuring DOMINIO IV COLUMBIA VALLEY SYRAH

1 Tbsp vegetable oil

½ medium onion, finely diced

1 small carrot, finely diced

3 cloves garlic, crushed

1 sprig fresh rosemary

½ Tbsp dried lavender

1½ cups Syrah

1 tsp sugar

½ cup strong dark-roast coffee

salt and freshly ground black pepper to taste

Looking for a great sauce for lamb, beef or game? Try this creation by Rob Leon of Phresh Organic Catering, which proved very popular at a winemakers' dinner. It uses the bold Columbia Valley Syrah with its fruity characteristics and wild floral aromas. The color is rich and dark and the tannin and acidity are well balanced.

1. Heat the oil in a saucepan over medium heat. Add the onion, carrot and garlic and season with a pinch or 2 of salt. Sauté until lightly golden, about 5–6 minutes.

2. Reduce the heat to low and add the rosemary and lavender. Cook, stirring often, until the herbs become fragrant, approximately 3–5 minutes.

3. Remove the saucepan from the heat and add the wine and sugar. Place the saucepan back on the stove, increase the heat to medium and reduce the liquid by half. Add the coffee and simmer together for about 3 minutes.

4. Remove from the heat, strain the liquid through a fine mesh strainer and set it aside. Remove the rosemary and discard it. Using a blender, purée the vegetables with just enough of the liquid to allow the blender to whirl.

5. Combine the purée and the reserved liquid and strain. Adjust the seasoning with sugar, salt and pepper and serve over your meat.

MAKES 1½–2 CUPS

DOMINIO IV
801 North Scott Street, Carlton
TEL: (503) 852-6100 or
1 (867) 877-7776
www.dominiowines.com
patrick@dominiowies.com

WINE SHOP, TOURS AND TASTINGS
Open 11 a.m.–5 p.m. daily and by
appointment in Feb. Tours on Sat. at
noon and 3 p.m.

GETTING THERE
Between Yamhill and McMinnville on
Highway 47, just north of town.

WINERY HIGHLIGHTS
The winery is part of Carlton
Winemakers Studio, a co-operative
venture where there are 10 wineries
making wines to sample.

Desserts

A hard drinker at the table was offered grapes at dessert. "Thank you," said he, pushing the plate away from him, "but I am not in the habit of taking my wine in pills."

—*Jean Anthelme Brillat-Savarin,* The Physiology of Taste

Champagne Creek Cellars Bittersweet Mocha Mousse

featuring HANS BLEND CABERNET SAUVIGNON

12 oz semi-sweet chocolate, chips or chopped

⅓ cup cold strong coffee

⅓ cup Cabernet Sauvignon

1 Tbsp rum

1 cup whipping cream

fresh berries for garnish

This simple recipe takes just minutes to prepare, yet it's so impressive. The wine is dark and complex, with a nose of toasty cherry pie and leather. The rich jammy mid-palate gives way to a long finish of cedar and bittersweet chocolate. It's perfect for this marvelous mocha.

1. Mix the chocolate, coffee, wine and rum in a blender.

2. Whip the cream until it thickens in a separate bowl.

3. Gently fold the blended ingredients into the cream.

4. Chill and serve with berries.

SERVES 8

CHAMPAGNE CREEK CELLARS

340 Busenbark Lane, Roseburg
TEL: (541) 673-7901
www.champagnecreek.com
info@champagnecreekcellars.com

WINE SHOP, TOURS AND TASTINGS

Tasting daily 11 a.m.–5 p.m. or
6 p.m. in the summer. Tours by
appointment.

GETTING THERE

Take exit 125 off the I-5. Go west and
veer left onto Melrose Road. Follow
for just over a mile, then turn right
onto Busenbark Lane. The driveway is
1 block up on the left.

WINERY HIGHLIGHTS

The winery has won more than
100 awards since its inception in
2001. Reds are a highlight, and
unusual wines are always being
introduced. A recent introduction
was a white Merlot.

Willamette Valley Cherries Poached in Syrah

featuring SYRAH

1½ lb fresh cherries

1½ cups Syrah

1½ cups water

½ cup brown sugar

4 tsp grated orange zest

Make this a day ahead and refrigerate it if you're pressed for time. The extra time in the juice will only increase the flavor. This would be a perfect end to a summer barbecue.

1. Remove the pits and stems from the cherries.

2. Mix the wine, water, sugar and orange zest in a saucepan over medium heat, and bring to a simmer.

3. Add the cherries and simmer for 6–7 minutes. Remove from the heat, cover and allow the cherries to cool. Let the cherries sit in the juice for 2–3 hours before serving. It's even better with some vanilla ice cream!

SERVES 4–6

Syrah

pronounced (SEE-RAHH)

This grape, known as Shiraz in South Africa and Australia, has a long history. Many historians believe it was originally grown in southern Iran, near the village of Shiraz, and was taken back to France by the crusaders some time between the 11th and 13th centuries. Others contend the grape has always been a native of France.

In France, the grape was originally grown in the Rhone Valley, where it was developed into the style of wine we have come to love. In Oregon it has continued to increase in popularity and more and more vineyards are planting this varietal.

Syrah buds rather late but ripens mid-season. The grape is thick skinned and very dark. The wine is usually deep violet in color and often has aromas and flavors of blackberry, pepper, herbs and cinnamon. Warm weather produces a fruitier wine and cooler seasons give it spicier aromas.

Syrah pairs well with heavy foods, such as lamb, steak, duck and game bird, and it's a guaranteed winner with just about anything that has been barbecued.

Silvan Ridge Pear Bread Pudding with Muscat Sauce

featuring SILVAN RIDGE EARLY MUSCAT SEMI-SPARKLING

1 Tbsp butter

3 Tbsp currants

1 large ripe pear, peeled, cored and cubed

½ cup Early Muscat

4 slices white bread, trimmed and cubed

1½ cups milk, scalded

12 egg yolks

⅔ cup sugar

1 cup milk

1 cup light cream

1 3-inch strip lemon zest

Fruity flavors of white peach, Asian pear and apricot glide across the palate on creamy delicate bubbles followed by a crisp, cleansing finish. This wine makes an excellent accompaniment to dessert or brunch. Use the egg whites to make yourself a healthy omelet for breakfast the next day.

1. Preheat the oven to 350°F. Butter 6 ramekins or molds for the puddings. In a small bowl, combine the currants, pear and ⅓ cup of the wine. Let stand for 30 minutes.

2. Place the bread cubes in a separate bowl. Pour the scalded milk over the bread and let it stand for 10 minutes. Gently beat 6 of the egg yolks and add to the bread mixture. Add the pear mixture and ⅓ cup of the sugar to the bread mixture and combine well. Divide the mixture among the ramekins and place them on a rack in a roasting pan. Pour boiling water into the roasting pan so that it comes about halfway up the sides of the ramekins. Bake for 40 minutes.

3. While the puddings are baking, make the sauce. Bring the milk, cream and lemon zest to a boil in a saucepan. Remove the saucepan immediately from the heat and let it stand for 5 minutes. In a large bowl combine the remaining ⅓ cup sugar and the remaining 6 egg yolks and beat until well blended. Remove the lemon zest and gradually pour the milk mixture into the yolks, stirring constantly with a wire whisk.

SILVAN RIDGE

27012 Briggs Hill Road, Eugene

TEL: (541) 345-1945

FAX: (541) 345-6174

www.silvanridge.com

info@silvanridge.com

WINE SHOP, TOURS AND TASTINGS
Open daily noon–5 p.m. There is no
charge for tasting featured wines.
Tours by appointment only.

GETTING THERE
From Eugene, take West 11th or West
18th Avenue to Bertelsen Road and
turn left. Turn right on Spencer Creek
Road and continue for about 3 miles.
Turn left on Briggs Hill Road. Turn left
at the winery entrance.

WINERY HIGHLIGHTS
Relax by the cozy fireplace, shop in
the tasting room or enjoy a picnic
on the patio. Only the best fruit
from established growers is used
to make their Pinot Noir, Pinot Gris,
Early Muscat, Chardonnay, Riesling,
Merlot, Syrah and Viognier.

4. Return the mixture to the saucepan and cook over low heat, stirring with a wooden spoon until the sauce thickens enough to coat the spoon. Do not boil! Remove from the heat and pour through a fine mesh strainer into a small bowl. Let it cool and then stir in the remaining wine.

5. The puddings are cooked when a knife inserted between the center and edge comes out clean. Let them stand for 5 minutes before unmolding. Serve with the sauce and enjoy with a glass of Silvan Ridge Early Muscat.

SERVES 6

Paradis Vineyard Pinot Noir Cobbler

featuring PARADIS VINEYARD PINOT NOIR

½ cup Pinot Noir

2 cups fresh berries (or use frozen)

2 tart apples, peeled, cored and sliced

¾ cup sugar plus 2 Tbsp sugar

1 Tbsp cornstarch

1 cup all-purpose flour

1 Tbsp baking powder

½ tsp salt

6 Tbsp cold butter

¼ cup buttermilk

½ cup whipping cream

Cobblers are great as you don't have to fiddle around rolling out pie dough or crust. The berries are the important part and Oregon has an abundance of these. The wine complements the berries with intriguing earthy aromas followed by strawberry shortcake, candied fruit and chili pepper flavors. Enjoy it now—it is a pleasure with food—but it will also age and mature well.

1. Preheat the oven to 425°F. Butter a 9-×13-inch baking dish. Combine the wine, berries, apples, ¾ cup sugar and cornstarch. Mix well and distribute evenly in the buttered pan.

2. Combine the flour, remaining 2 Tbsp sugar, baking powder and salt in a large bowl. Cut in the butter until the mixture resembles coarse meal. Gently fold in the buttermilk; do not overmix. Drop the batter in spoonfuls over the fruit.

3. Bake for 40 minutes or until the fruit is bubbling and the crust is brown. Have a glass of Paradis Pinot Noir while waiting for the dessert to bake.

4. Allow the cobbler to cool slightly before serving with the cream.

SERVES 8

PARADIS VINEYARD
17627 Abiqua Road, Silverton
TEL: (503) 873-8475
www.paradiswine.com
donna@paradiswine.com

WINE SHOP, TOURS AND TASTINGS
Open Memorial and Thanksgiving
weekends as well as every second
Sat. of the month for East Valley
Wine Tour "Second Saturday" events.
Private tastings by appointment.
Phone for details.

GETTING THERE
On Highway 213, between mile
markers 26 and 27 is Abiqua Road
N. Turn east on Abiqua Road N and
drive 2 miles to the vineyard.

WINERY HIGHLIGHTS
Located in the picturesque Abiqua
Valley. Enjoy the wines and hear the
vintners tell their story. Paradis is a
family-owned and -run operation and
uses environmentally safe practices
to tend to the vines. Their goal is to
craft small lots of quality wine at an
affordable price.

WINERY SPECIAL OFFER
Show your copy of this book to
receive a complimentary Paradis
Vineyard logo glass.

Mango, Strawberry and Basil Bruschetta

featuring GEWÜRZTRAMINER

½ cup Gewürztraminer

1 Tbsp lime juice

1 Tbsp sugar

1 ripe mango, diced

½ lb strawberries, diced

1 Tbsp finely chopped fresh
basil

3 Tbsp butter, softened

3 Tbsp brown sugar

1 tsp ground cinnamon

24 baguette slices (¼–½ inch
thick)

Bruschetta (correctly pronounced brus-ket-ah, not brush-et-ah) originated in central Italy and is usually served as an appetizer or snack. With some help from our friends we've come up with this dessert version, which is also delicious for a breakfast treat. If you don't have much time or want a healthier treat, try the fruit mixture on its own.

1. Combine the wine, lime juice and sugar in a small saucepan over medium heat, stirring until the sugar dissolves. Simmer until the liquid is reduced by half. When you have about ¼ cup liquid, remove from the heat and chill.

2. Mix the mango, strawberries, basil and chilled wine mixture in a medium-sized bowl. Cover and refrigerate.

3. Mix the butter, sugar and cinnamon in a small bowl until you have a smooth paste. Spread the mixture thinly on 1 side of each baguette slice.

4. Place under the broiler, buttered side up, for about 2 minutes, until the topping is bubbly and the bread is lightly browned on the edges.

5. Spoon a small amount of the fruit mixture on each baguette slice and serve immediately.

SERVES 6—8

Gewürztraminer

pronounced (GAA-VERTS-TRA-MEE-NER)

Wine historians disagree on the meaning and origins of the word Gewürztraminer. However, most report that the name comes from **gewurz**, *a German word meaning "spicy," and* **Traminer**, *which is a variety of grape.*

Traminer comes from the Italian village of Termeno, located in Germany's Tyrolean Alps. The grape had been growing very successfully there since the Middle Ages. Some time in the last few hundred years it mutated into the grape we know as Gewürztraminer. Today it's commonly grown in the Alsace region of France.

Gewürztraminer was among the first varieties planted in Oregon by Richard Sommer in the early 1960s. It grows well here and has distinct aromatic characteristics of flowers and spicy perfumes, similar to Muscat. The wine can be stored for a few years without problems, but it's best when consumed young.

Gewürztraminer is a great accompaniment for a wide variety of foods. It is especially good with spicy foods, stone fruits, game, poultry and cheese.

Cooper Mountain Panna Cotta with Rhubarb Lemoncello Compote

featuring COOPER MOUNTAIN PINOT BLANC VIN GLACE

8 cups whipping cream

1 vanilla bean

1½ cups sugar

7 sheets gelatin (if using powdered gelatin, this is about 2 envelopes)

2 Tbsp butter

6 rhubarb stalks (the larger and redder the better), cut in ½-inch pieces

½ cup white dessert wine

2 Tbsp fresh lemon juice

1 cinnamon stick

1-3 Tbsp grenadine for color

This sweet but balanced dessert wine is a big favorite among Cooper Mountain's customers. Made in an icewine style from artificially frozen Pinot Blanc grapes, the Vin Glace always sells out fast. It adds a delicious flavor to this scrumptious dessert and provides an amazing pairing. This recipe can be easily halved or doubled.

1. Place the cream in a large saucepan. Scrape the seeds from the vanilla bean into the cream and toss the bean in as well. Add 1 cup of the sugar.

2. Scald the mixture over medium-high heat, bringing it almost to a boil, but making sure not to boil it. Reduce the heat. Add the gelatin sheets 1 at a time, whisking after each addition to make sure it's fully incorporated.

3. Remove the vanilla bean and pour the mixture into individual 8-oz ramekins or molds. Chill for 1–2 hours. While it is chilling start the compote.

4. Melt the butter in a pot over medium heat. Add the rhubarb, remaining ½ cup of sugar, wine, lemon juice, cinnamon stick and grenadine. Simmer and stir until it's the consistency of a purée. Taste and if you prefer it sweeter, add a little more sugar.

5. Run a paring knife around the inside of the ramekins and turn out the panna cotta onto serving plates. Garnish with as much compote as you wish. Enjoy the dish with a chilled glass of Cooper Mountain Vineyard Pinot Blanc Vin Glace.

SERVES 10

COOPER MOUNTAIN VINEYARD
9480 SW Grabhorn Road, Beaverton
TEL: (503) 649-0027
FAX: (503) 649-0702
www.coopermountainwine.com
info@coopermountainwine.com

WINE SHOP, TOURS AND TASTINGS
Tasting room open daily noon–
5 p.m. Groups are welcome and
appointments are appreciated.

GETTING THERE
From Highway 26W head toward
Beaverton and merge onto OR
217 S, exit 69A. Take the OR-8/
Canyon Road/OR 10, exit 2A (the
road has three names) heading
toward Beaverton. Turn right onto
SW Canyon Road, then left onto
Grabhorn Road/209th.

WINERY HIGHLIGHTS
This is Oregon's first organic and
biodynamic winery. All the wines
are estate bottled. Picnic tables are
available. Check the website for
special events.

Eugene Wine Cellars Wine Mousse

featuring PENDARVINE WILLAMETTE VALLEY PINOT NOIR

1 cup Pinot Noir

1 cup water

1 tsp fresh lemon juice

½ cup sugar

⅓ cup cornstarch

1 egg yolk

⅔ cup whipping cream

This traditional German dessert can be prepared well in advance of dinner. It will hold up in the refrigerator for 1 to 2 days. The dark ruby wine has aromas of blackcurrant and berry. Fruit flavors include strawberry and dark cherry. It is excellent served with salmon, pork, beef, poultry or a simple plate of bread and cheese.

1. Slowly heat up the wine, water and lemon juice in a medium-sized pot. In a separate bowl combine the sugar, cornstarch and egg yolk with a wire whisk. Stir into the pot and make sure you do not bring it to a boil. Keep stirring and after about 5 minutes the mixture will become thick.

2. Transfer the mixture to a bowl. Put that bowl inside another larger bowl filled with ice-cold water, or even better, ice cubes. Stir the mixture with a wire whisk until it cools down to below room temperature.

3. In a separate bowl beat the cream until it's fluffy. Carefully fold or mix it into the wine mixture. Transfer to 4 small bowls or serving dishes and refrigerate for 2 hours before serving.

SERVES 4

EUGENE WINE CELLARS

255 Madison Street, Eugene
TEL: (541) 342-2600
FAX: (541) 341-1132
www.eugenewinecellars.com
office@eugenewinecellars.com

WINE SHOP, TOURS AND TASTINGS

Tasting room open Mon.–Fri.
10 a.m.–4 p.m., Sat. 1 p.m.–7 p.m.
and by appointment. No tasting fee
is charged.

GETTING THERE

Exit off I-5 onto I-105W/OR 126
via exit 194B toward Eugene. Take
the OR 99N/OR 126 exit toward
Florence. Turn right onto Madison
Street. The winery is 3 blocks down
the street on your right, past the
train tracks.

WINERY HIGHLIGHTS

An urban winery in the midst of
Eugene, EWC sources its fruit from
independent vineyards whose
day-to-day operations are managed
by the winery owner's vineyard
management company (AREA). This
ensures that only the highest quality
of grapes are used.

Foris Vineyards Berry-Port Cake

featuring FORIS PORT

½ cup blackberries

¾ cup raspberries

¼ cup port

1 cup sugar

½ cup butter, softened

2 large eggs

1 cup all-purpose flour

1 tsp baking powder

vanilla ice cream or sweetened
   whipped cream

Port and berries combine beautifully in this elegant dessert that will have your guests begging you for the recipe. The grapes for this Cabernet Sauvignon Port come from Del Rio Vineyard in the warmer eastern reach of the Rogue Valley AVA. High-quality Oregon-produced grape brandy was added to kill off the yeast and end fermentation. It has a mouth-watering, lingering finish of currants, plums and raisins.

1. Preheat the oven to 350°F. Butter and flour a 9-inch springform pan.

2. Gently mix the blackberries, ½ cup of the raspberries, port and 1 Tbsp of the sugar in a bowl. Set aside.

3. Use a mixer on high speed to beat the remaining sugar and the butter for 2–3 minutes, until well blended. Add the eggs and beat for another 2–3 minutes until fluffy. Add the flour and baking powder. Stir to combine, then beat on high speed for about 2 minutes until the batter is well blended (it will be stiff). Scrape the batter into the cake pan and smooth the top.

4. Drain the wine marinade from the berries and reserve. Evenly spoon the berries and 2 Tbsp of the marinade over the batter.

FORIS VINEYARDS WINERY
654 Kendall Road, Cave Junction
TEL: (541) 592-3752 or
1 (800) 843-6747
FAX: (541) 592-4424
www.foriswine.com
foris@foriswine.com

WINE SHOP, TOURS AND TASTINGS
Tasting room open 11 a.m.–5 p.m.
daily. No charge for tasting.

GETTING THERE
From I-5 take exit 55 in Grants
Pass (Highway 199) south to Cave
Junction. In Cave Junction, turn left
onto Highway 46 toward Oregon
Caves. Proceed about 6½ miles to
Holland Loop. Turn right on Holland
Loop and proceed about 2½ miles
to the Holland Store. Turn left at
Kendall Road.

WINERY HIGHLIGHTS
The covered area in the vineyard is a
perfect spot to enjoy your picnic and
a glass of Foris Wine.

5. Bake for 50–55 minutes (40–45 minutes in a
convection oven) until the cake begins to pull away
from the pan rim. Remove from the oven and run a
thin-bladed knife between the cake and pan. Let it cool
for at least 30 minutes.

6. Remove the pan rim and sprinkle the cake with a little
more sugar. Top with the remaining ¼ cup raspberries.
Cut into wedges and moisten each portion with the
reserved wine marinade. Accompany with scoops of
ice cream or sweetened whipped cream. Delicious
when served with Foris Port.

SERVES 6—8

Ponzi's Poached Pears

featuring PONZI VINO GELATO

4 fresh, firm pears (preferably Bartlett)

½ cup mild, soft goat cheese

½ cup chopped hazelnuts

1½ cups icewine (or white dessert wine)

1 cup water

1 vanilla bean

white sugar to taste

Nancy Ponzi says: "Pears, especially whole, poached in wine, are a classic harvest season dessert. Combining this classic with our Vino Gelato creates a distinct and delicious Ponzi version. The fact the preparation is simple and almost foolproof makes it especially endearing."

1. Carefully peel and core the pears. Combine the cheese with the nuts and fill the center of the pears with the mixture.

2. Bring the wine and water to a boil in a wide, flat saucepan. Reduce the heat to a simmer. Split the vanilla bean and scrape the seeds into the liquid. Add the pears and simmer until just tender, about 8–10 minutes.

3. Gently remove the pears with a slotted spoon. Set aside to cool or put directly into serving dishes. Here is a great chance to use those old, flat champagne glasses!

4. Simmer the liquid for 10–15 minutes to make a sauce for the pears. Taste and add sugar if more sweetness is desired. Garnish the pears with the sauce just before serving.

SERVES 4

PONZI VINEYARDS

14665 SW Winery Lane, Beaverton
TEL: (503) 628-1227
FAX: (503) 628-0354
www.ponziwines.com
info@ponziwines.com

WINE SHOP, TOURS AND TASTINGS
Open daily 11 a.m.–5 p.m. A variety of
custom tour packages are available
by appointment.

GETTING THERE
From Portland, take I-5 south to exit
292 and turn right onto Highway 217.
Take the Scholls Ferry/Progress exit
to Scholls Ferry Road and turn left.
Follow Scholls Ferry Road until you
see the Ponzi Vineyards Winery sign
and turn left onto Vandermost Road.
This will take you to Winery Lane
and the Ponzi Winery. Travel time is
about 35 minutes.

WINERY HIGHLIGHTS
Enjoy the winery's lawn, patio and
bocce ball court areas during the
summer months. Visitors may taste
the current wines and stroll through
one of the region's oldest vineyards.
There is also an elegant space for
private events.

Ribbon Ridge Vineyards Chocolate Lavender Torte with Muscat Sabayon

featuring DEWEY KELLY EARLY MUSCAT FROM RIBBON RIDGE VINEYARD

2 cups Early Muscat

1 cup broken-up chocolate wafers

¼ cup melted butter

6 oz semi-sweet chocolate

¾ cup butter

1¼ cups sugar

12 egg yolks

½ tsp dried lavender

6 egg whites

pinch of salt

Ribbon Ridge produces the Dewey Kelly Early Muscat in very small quantities. Floral peach and apricot aromatics are embellished by a silky smooth texture. The frizzante style adds a touch of fun.

1. Preheat the oven to 325°F. In a small saucepan over high heat reduce 1 cup of the wine to ¼ cup. Set aside for later use.

2. Place the chocolate wafers in a food processor and process to fine crumbs. Add the melted butter and process briefly. Pat the crumbs onto the bottom of a 9-inch springform pan (do not grease).

3. Combine the chocolate, butter and ¾ cup of the sugar in a double boiler over simmering water. Melt and blend well, then remove from the heat. Mix in 6 egg yolks, lavender and the reduced wine.

4. In a separate bowl, beat the egg whites with the salt until firm peaks form. Fold the whites into the chocolate mixture. Scoop the mixture over the chocolate crust. Bake for 40 minutes. Allow the torte to cool before removing from the pan.

5. Whisk together the remaining ½ cup sugar, 1 cup Early Muscat and the remaining 6 egg yolks in a large stainless steel bowl. Set the bowl over barely simmering water. Whisk constantly until the mixture thickens and reads 160°F on a thermometer. Serve warm, or cool it by whisking over a bowl of ice.

6. Cut the cake in 10–12 portions and spoon the Muscat sabayon over each piece. Fresh fruit is a nice addition.

SERVES 10–12

RIBBON RIDGE AT CARLTON
WINEMAKERS STUDIO
801 N Scott Street, Carlton
Ribbon Ridge
TEL: (503) 502-5255
FAX: (503) 452-0258
www.ribbonridge.com

CARLTON WINEMAKERS STUDIO
TEL: (503) 852-6100
FAX: (503) 852-9519
www.winemakersstudio.com
info@winemakersstudio.com

WINE SHOP, TOURS AND TASTINGS
Carlton Winemakers Studio is open
Feb.–Dec., daily 11 a.m.–5 p.m. Tasting
fees range from complimentary to $6.

GETTING THERE
Carlton Winemakers Studio is 45
minutes southwest of Portland. Take
Highway 99W to Newberg, Highway
240 to Yamhill, then turn left on
Highway 47 and continue for 3 miles.
CWS is on the right.

WINERY HIGHLIGHTS
CWS is home to 10 small, remarkable
wineries producing 40+ wines. The
state of the art, eco-friendly co-
operative is the first of its kind in
the United States.

Muscat

pronounced (MOOS-CAHT)

The Muscat family of grapes is generally recognized as one of the oldest in the world, so it's not surprising it's also one of the largest. More than 200 varieties of Muscat are grown worldwide.

The grape reportedly takes its name from an ancient sultanate near present-day Oman (today the capital of Oman is called Muscat). It's possible this is where the grape originated; however, Greece seems more likely.

These days the grape is grown everywhere, and Oregon is no exception. Varieties of Muscat grown in the Pacific Northwest include Early Muscat (becoming very popular), Black Muscat, Orange Muscat, Muscat Caneli and Muscat Ottonel among others.

The aroma of Muscat wine is often very similar to the aroma of the grape itself. If you're in a vineyard, give the grapes a good sniff, remember the fragrance and then smell the wine. The ancient Roman Pliny, in his **Natural History,** *written around AD 77, declared the varietal "the grape of the bees" because of its overpowering scent.*

There are so many different styles of Muscat that it's difficult to find common characteristics. The wines can be sparkling or still and in Oregon they usually range from off-dry to sweet. They're generally food friendly and go very well with seafood or Asian dishes.

Drinks

The world needs water. For every bottle
of wine you drink you contribute to
conserving the drinking water reserve.

—Paul Emil Victor, polar explorer

Champoeg Mimosas

featuring CHAMPOEG CHARDONNAY RESERVE

½ glass pulp-free orange juice
½ glass Chardonnay

Mimosas are usually made with sparkling wine. They are a family favorite of ours on Christmas morning and other special occasions. Champoeg Cellars have come up with this alternative to the common mimosa by using their Chardonnay Reserve in place of sparkling wine.

1. Pour the orange juice into a stemmed wineglass. Add the wine and fill right to the brim.

2. That's it, you're done. Sit back and enjoy your refreshing wine cocktail.

SERVES 1

Gavino!

featuring PINOT NOIR

1 oz gin (preferably Bombay Sapphire)
½ oz crème de cassis
2 oz Pinot Noir
½ lime, quartered
2 tsp white sugar

Cocktail guru Gavin Forbes of Company Bar in the UK has developed this incredible beverage especially for this book. Featuring plump blueberries and Pinot Noir, this drink could soon become an Oregon institution.

1. Combine all the ingredients in a cocktail shaker and muddle them together (to muddle you crush all the ingredients together using a wooden muddler or the back of a spoon).

2. Add ice and shake well before straining into a highball glass filled with crushed ice. Garnish with extra blueberries.

SERVES 1

CHAMPOEG WINE CELLARS

10375 Champoeg Road NE, Aurora
TEL: (503) 678-2144
FAX: (503) 678-1024
www.champoegwine.com
champoeg@champoegwine.com

WINE SHOP, TOURS AND TASTINGS
Tasting room open Thu.–Mon.
11 a.m.–5 p.m. Closed Tue.–Wed.,
also closed Easter, Thanksgiving,
Christmas and New Year's Day.
Tastings and tours are free.

GETTING THERE
Travel south on I-5 past Wilsonville.
Take exit 282A (after crossing the
Willamette River on I-5 there are
2 exits; 282A is the second exit).
This will take you under the freeway
heading south. After 1½ miles take a
right at the traffic light on to Arndt
Road. Travel west to Butteville and
stay on the main road as it meanders
down and through Butteville; ¼ mile
after Butteville, take a right on
Champoeg Road. The winery is
½ mile farther on the right.

WINERY HIGHLIGHTS
Visitors can view both the
vineyard and winery activities
through the large tasting room
windows. Bring a picnic and enjoy
the view of Mt. Hood.

Sparkling Sherbet Spritzer

featuring SPARKLING WINE

1 scoop sherbet (any flavor)
1 glass sparkling wine

Marilyn Blen of Kramer Vineyards has come up with this easy and simple recipe that can be enjoyed as an after-dinner treat or out on the deck during a hot afternoon. She used the Kramer Vineyards Sparkling Müller-Thurgau.

1. Place a scoop of sherbet in a large wineglass.

2. Top up the glass with sparkling wine. It will foam and fizz a lot.

SERVES 1

Sparkling Wine

"It's like drinking the stars!" exclaimed Benedictine monk Dom Perignon as he sipped on a glass of champagne. Champagne is named for the region in France where sparkling wine achieved worldwide fame. All wine that undergoes a second fermentation, carbonation, is called sparkling wine. International law forbids most other wine regions from using the term "champagne" to label sparkling wine, although in Washington many wineries use the same methods as those employed in France to make the bubbly beverage. These are usually labeled "méthode champenoise" or "fermented in this bottle."

Other countries have created their own regional names to distinguish their versions of this festive drink. It is called "cava" in Spain, "spumante" in Italy and "sekt" in Germany and Austria.

Sparkling wine should be served chilled. This can be done quickly by placing the bottle in a sink full of ice and water. When opening a bottle of sparkling wine, carefully remove the foil cage, being sure not to point the bottle at anyone. Then grip the cork firmly and gently turn the bottle, easing the cork free.

The aroma should be clean and fresh, and citrus notes in the wine are usually a good sign. The smaller the bubbles the better, as they create a creamy sensation as opposed to the "soda water fizz" created by large bubbles.

Sparkling wine is often consumed only on special occasions, but this need not be the case as it pairs well with most types of food. It's especially wonderful at breakfast and it's well worth investing in a sparkling wine sealer so you can save some of the previous night's bottle especially for this reason.

SakéOne's G-Sling Sakétini

featuring G-Joy (Junmai Ginjo Saké)

2 oz G-Joy Saké

1 oz banana rum (preferably Cruzan)

½ oz fresh lemon juice

½ oz lime juice

1 oz simple syrup

Wine and saké expert Dewey Weddington gives us his favorite saketini using the G-Joy Saké. G is for Genshu. In saké speak, this means premium grade and cask strength, typically 18–21 percent alcohol by volume. G-Joy is 18 percent, but the character and body are mellow and balance the alcohol levels, leaving a smooth, clean beverage that's highly pleasurable to drink.

1. Combine all the ingredients in a cocktail shaker with ice and shake vigorously.

2. Serve on the rocks with a slice of lime and a tropical flower.

SERVES 1

SAKÉ ONE

820 Elm Street, Forest Grove
TEL: (503) 357-7056
FAX: (503) 357-1014
www.sakeone.com
info@sakeone.com

WINE SHOP, TOURS AND TASTINGS
Tasting room open daily noon–5 p.m.
A $3 tasting fee includes up
to 5 tastes of premium saké.
Complimentary tours at 1 p.m.,
2 p.m. and 3 p.m. daily.

GETTING THERE
Located about 30 minutes west of
Portland and just South of Forest
Grove on Highway 47.

WINERY HIGHLIGHTS
This is the only American-owned
and -operated sakéry in the world.
Sakétini Saturday is every third
Saturday of every month.

BARTENDER'S TIP

It's easy to make your own simple syrup. Just mix 1 part water and 1½ parts sugar in a saucepan and boil until the sugar has dissolved. Now transfer to a bottle and you have a ready-made cocktail bar ingredient!

Bendistillery Bellini

featuring CRATER LAKE VODKA

3 oz vodka

3 oz white peach purée

1 oz sparkling wine

Yes, we know, this is not a winery! But while wine touring in Oregon, we figured you might want a little change once in a while. Of course, there is still wine in the recipe and this simple cocktail makes a refreshing treat on a hot afternoon. The drink was invented at Harry's Bar in Venice, Italy.

1. Mix the vodka and the white peach purée in a cocktail shaker over ice. Shake lightly.

2. Strain the mixture into a champagne flute and top with the sparkling wine.

3. We guarantee you will not want to stop at just one.

SERVES 1

BENDISTILLERY

1470 NE 1st Street, Suite 800, Bend
Sampling Room:
850 NW Brooks Street, Bend
TEL: (541) 318-0200
FAX: (541) 318-1886
www.bendistillery.com
aland@bendistillery.com

TOURS AND TASTINGS
Martini bar and sampling room open
Tue.–Sat. 4 p.m.–midnight.

GETTING THERE
Sampling room is located in
downtown Bend on the Brooks Street
alley just down from the historic
Pine Tavern on the Mirror Pond Plaza
overlooking Drake Park and the
Deschutes River.

WINERY HIGHLIGHTS
The gins and vodkas are made
from only the freshest, all-natural
ingredients and are created with an
attention to quality that can only
be achieved through small hand-
crafted batches. In fact, each batch
is numbered on the bottle and every
bottle is autographed.

Winery Listings & Maps

WINE IS MUCH MORE THAN JUST A DRINK—WINE IS ABOUT people, places and culture. To help you meet those people, discover those places and share that culture, we've gathered together information on all the wineries in Oregon and included it in this section, along with maps that will help you discover the magnificent terroir.

We've divided the state into separate areas to make the maps more useful and manageable. If you're looking for information on a particular winery but aren't sure which area it's in, consult the index.

Despite our best efforts to provide up-to-date information, it's important to remember that new wineries are constantly opening and existing wineries may adjust their hours of operation, close down or change their names. Every effort has been made to include complete and accurate information about every winery operating in Oregon, but to avoid disappointment it pays to call in advance when you plan to visit a winery.

Wine touring is an enjoyable way to explore the country and taste the fruits of the land, but we always recommend having a designated driver. A great way to reward your driver is to treat them to lunch at a winery or buy them a bottle or two of the wines you've tried that day.

The wine industry in Oregon is worth more than $1.4 billion annually and supports in excess of 8,000 jobs. The wineries scattered throughout the state each have their own unique personality. The wines themselves provide some insight, but there's no better way to understand the diversity of the industry than to visit the wineries yourself, talk to the people who make the wine and let their passion inspire you. Every winery has a unique story and discovering that story is often fascinating.

Driving Distances

(Approximate times with good driving conditions)

With more than 250 wineries currently in operation, there's a lot to see and taste. The diverse wine landscapes, ranging from awe-inspiring coastline to majestic mountain slopes, from lush river valleys to bustling cities, make the journey every bit as enjoyable as the tasting. Your adventure is just beginning, so get out there and enjoy the spectacular, winding wine roads of Oregon.

ASHLAND – CORVALLIS: 225 miles, 3 hrs 45 min

ASHLAND – EUGENE: 180 miles, 3 hrs

ASHLAND – PORTLAND: 285 miles, 4 hrs 45 min

BEND – CORVALLIS: 130 miles, 2 hrs 45 min

CARLTON – MCMINNVILLE: 8 miles, 20 min

CORVALLIS – PORTLAND: 85 miles, 1 hr 40 min

CORVALLIS – EUGENE: 50 miles, 1 hr

THE DALLES – HOOD RIVER: 25 miles, 30 min

EUGENE – SALEM: 65 miles, 1 hr 15 min

EUGENE – ROSEBURG: 75 miles, 1 hr 15 min

HOOD RIVER – PORTLAND: 65 miles, 1 hr 15 min

NEWBERG – MCMINNVILLE: 15 miles, 30 min

MEDFORD – CAVE JUNCTION: 60 miles, 1 hr 15 min

MCMINNVILLE – HOOD RIVER: 100 miles, 2 hrs 15 min

PORTLAND – CARLTON: 40 miles, 1 hr 15 min

PORTLAND – FOREST GROVE: 25 miles, 40 min

SEATTLE – PORTLAND: 170 miles, 3 hrs

SALEM – CARLTON: 30 miles, 1 hr

SAN FRANCISCO – ASHLAND: 350 miles, 6 hrs

Wineries of the North Willamette Valley

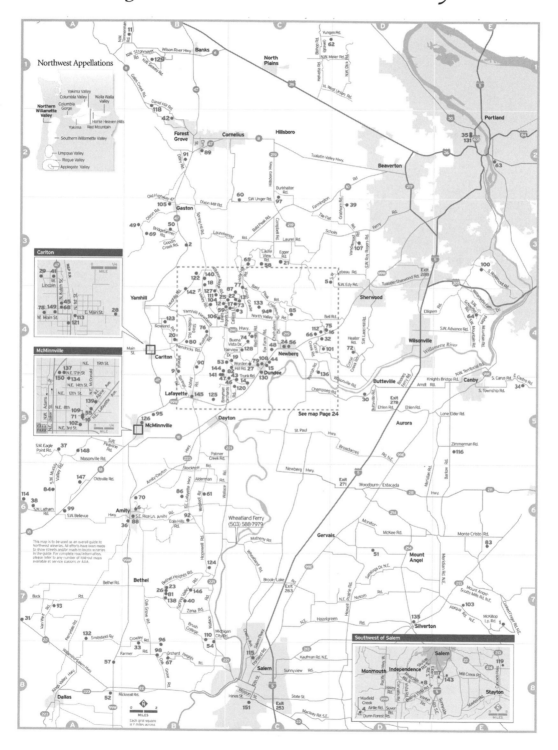

Wineries

1. Abiqua Wind Vineyard	E7	26. Bryn Mawr Vineyards	B7	51. Engelhardt Farm	D6	76. Laurel Ridge Winery	B4, A2	101. Owen Roe	C4, C2	126. Stone Wolf Vineyards	B5
2. ADEA Wine Co.	B3	27. Cameron Winery	C4, B3	52. Eola Hills Wine Cellars	A8	77. Lawton Winery	C4, B1	102. Panther Creek Cellars	A5	127. Styring Vineyards	B4, A1
3. Adelsheim Vineyard	C4, B1	28. Carlo & Julian Winery	A4	53. Erath Vineyards	C4, A3	78. Lazy River Vineyard	A4	103. Paradis Family Vineyard	E7	128. Torii Mor Winery	C4, B2
4. Airlie Winery	D8	29. Carlton Winemakers Studio	A3	54. Evesham Wood Winery	B7	79. Le Cadeau Vineyard	C4, B3	104. Patricia Green Cellars	B4, A1	129. Tualatin Estate Vineyards	B1
5. Alloro Vineyard	D3, C1	30. Champoeg Wine Cellars	D5	55. The Eyrie Vineyards	A5	80. Lemelson Vineyards	B4, A4	105. Patton Valley Vineyard	B3	130. Twelfth & Maple Wine Co.	C4, B3
6. Amity Vineyards	B6	31. Chateau Bianca Winery	A7	56. Ferraro Cellar	C4, C2	81. Lewman Vineyard	B7	106. Penner-Ash Wine Cellars	B4, A2	131. Urban Wineworks	E2
7. Anderson Family Vineyard	C4, B2	32. Chehalem	C4, C2	57. Firesteed Cellars	A8	82. Maresh Red Barn	C4, B3	107. Ponzi Vineyards	D3	132. Van Duzer Vineyards	A7
8. Ankeny Vineyard Winery	D8	33. Cherry Hill Winery	B7	58. Freja Cellars	C3	83. Marquam Hill Vineyards	E6	108. Ponzi Wine Bar	C4, B3	133. Vidon Vineyard	C4, B1
9. Anne Amie Vineyards	B4, A3	34. Christopher Bridge Cellars	E5	59. Grochau Cellars	C4, A1	84. Maysara Estate Winery	A6	109. R. Stuart & Co.	A5	134. Viento	A5
10. Anthony Dell Cellars	A5	35. Clear Creek Distillery	E2	60. Gypsy Dancer Estate	C3	85. Medici Vineyards and Winery	C4, C1	110. Redhawk Winery	B7	135. Vitis Ridge/Silverton Cellars	D7
11. Apolloni/Ruby Carbiener	B1	36. Coelho Winery	B6	61. Hauer of the Dauen	B6	86. Methven Family Wines	B6	111. Redman Vineyard & Winery	B4, A1	136. VX/Vercingetorix	C4, C3
12. Aramenta Cellars	B4, A1	37. Coeur de Terre Vineyard	A5	62. Helvetia Vineyards and Winery	D1	87. Mia Jové Cellars	C4, B1	112. Rex Hill Vineyards	C4, C2	137. Walnut City WineWorks	A4
13. ArborBrook Vineyards	C4, B1	38. Coleman Vineyard	A6	63. Hip Chicks Do Wine	E2	88. Mia Sonatina Cellars	B6	113. Scott Paul Wines	A4	138. Wandering Aengus	B7
14. Archery Summit Winery	C5, B3	39. Cooper Mountain Vineyards	D3	64. Holloran Vineyard Wines	E4	89. SakéOne	B2	114. Seufert Winery	A6	139. Westrey Wine Co.	A5
15. Argyle Winery	C4, B3	40. Cristom Vineyards	B7	65. J. Albin Winery	C3	90. Monks Gate	B4, A3	115. St. Innocent Winery	C8	140. Whistling Ridge Vineyards	B3, A1
16. August Cellars	C4, C2	41. Cuneo Cellars	A4	66. J.K. Carriere Winery	C4, C2	91. Montinore Estate	B2	116. St. Josef's Wine Cellar	E5	141. White Rose Wines	B4, A3
17. Ayres Vineyard	C4, B1	42. David Hill Vineyard & Winery	B2	67. Kathken Vineyards	B8	92. Mystic Wines	B6	117. Sass Winery	E8	142. WillaKenzie Estate	B4, A1
18. Beaux Frères	B3, A1	43. De Ponte Cellars	C5, A3	68. Ken Wright Cellars	A4	93. Namasté Vineyards	A7	118. Shafer Vineyard Cellars	B1	143. Willamette Valley Vineyards	E8
19. Bella Vida Vineyard	C4, A3	44. Dobbes Family Estate	C4, B3	69. Kramer Vineyards	B3	94. Natalie's Estate Winery	C4, B1	119. Silver Falls Vineyards	E8	144. Wine Country Farm Cellars	B4, A3
20. Belle Pente Vineyard	B4	45. Domaine Coteau	A4	70. Kristin Hill Winery	B6	95. NW Wine Co.	B6	120. Sokol Blosser Winery	C5, B3	145. Winter's Hill Vineyard	B5, A3
21. Beran Vineyards	C3	46. Domaine Drouhin Oregon	C5, A3	71. La Bete Wines	A5	96. Oak Grove Orchards Winery	B8	121. Soléna Cellars	A4	146. Witness Tree Vineyard	B7
22. Bergström Winery	C4, B1	47. Domaine Serene	C4, A3	72. La Bonne Terre Vineyard	A4	97. Oak Knoll Winery	C2	122. Soter Vineyards	B3, A1	147. Yamhill Valley Vineyards	A6
23. Bethel Heights Vineyard	B7	48. Duck Pond Cellars	C4, B2	73. Lachini Vineyards	C4, B1	98. Orchard Heights Winery	B8	123. Stag Hollow Wines	B4	148. Youngberg Hill Vineyards & Inn	A5
24. Bishop Creek Cellars	C4, B2	49. Elk Cove Vineyards	B3	74. Lange Estate Winery	C4, B2	99. Oregon Wine Tasting Room	A6	124. Stangeland Vineyards	B7	149. Zenas Wines /150. Z'ivo Wines	A4
25. Brick House Vineyards	C4, A1	50. ElvenGlade Vineyard	B3	75. Laura Volkman Vineyards	C4, C2	100. Oswego Hills Winery	E3	125. Stoller Vineyards	B5, A3	151. Honeywood Winery	C8

WINERIES OF THE NORTH WILLAMETTE VALLEY

A TO Z
Dundee
(503) 864 4489
www.atozwineworks.com
Hours: Not open to the public

ABIQUA WIND
19822 McKillop Loop Road NE, Scott Mills
(503) 874 9818
Hours: Call for details

ACME WINEWORKS/THOMAS
Carlton
(503) 852 6969
Hours: Call for details

ADEA WINE COMPANY
26423 NW Highway 47, Gaston
(503) 662 4509
www.adeawine.com
Hours: By appointment

ADELSHEIM VINEYARD
16800 NE Calkins Lane, Newberg
(503) 538 3652
www.adelsheim.com
Hours: Memorial Day-Thanksgiving weekend by appointment

AGATE RIDGE VINEYARD, LLC
1098 Nick Young Road, Eagle Point
(541) 830 3050
www.agateridgevineyard.com
Hours: Call for hours

AIRLIE WINERY AND DUNN FOREST VINEYARD
15305 Dunn Forest Road, Monmouth
(503) 838 6013
www.airliewinerry.com
Hours: Weekends noon-5 p.m. or by appointment. Closed Easter, Thanksgiving and Christmas Day

ALLORO VINEYARD
22075 SW Lebeau Road, Sherwood
(503) 813 0063
www.allorovineyard.com
Hours: By appointment

AMITY VINEYARDS
18150 Amity Vineyards Road, Amity
1 (888) 264 8966
www.amityvineyards.com
Hours: By appointment

ANAM CARA CELLARS
(at August Cellars), Newberg
(503) 537 9150
www.anamcaracellars.com
Hours: May-Sep., daily 11 a.m.-5 p.m.; Oct.-Apr., weekends only or by appointment

ANDERSON FAMILY VINEYARD
20120 NE Herring Lane, Newberg
(503) 554 5541
Hours: By appointment

ANDREW RICH WINES
At Carlton Winemakers Studio, Carlton
(503) 284 6622
www.andrewrichwines.com
Hours: Open daily 11 a.m.-5 p.m. Tours on Sat. noon and 3 p.m. Closed Jan.

ANKENY VINEYARDS WINERY
2565 Riverside Road S, Salem
(503) 378 1498
www.ankenyvineyard.com
Hours: Memorial Day-Christmas, weekends noon-5 p.m.

ANNE AMIE VINEYARDS
6580 NE Mineral Springs Road, Carlton
(503) 864 2991
www.anneamie.com
Hours: Daily 10 a.m.-5 p.m.

ANTHONY DELL CELLARS
845 NE 5th Street Suite 300, McMinnville
(503) 910 8874
www.anthonydellcellars.com
Hours: Memorial Day Weekend and Thanksgiving weekends noon-5 p.m.

ANTHONY DELL CELLARS TASTING ROOM
610 Marion Street NE, Salem
(503) 910 8874
www.anthonydellcellars.com
Hours: Wed.-Sat. noon-6 p.m.

ANTICA TERRA
Portland
(503) 452 5369
www.anticaterra.com
Hours: By appointment

APOLLONI VINEYARDS
14135 NW Timmerman Road,
Forest Grove
(503) 330 5946
www.apolloni.com
Hours: Fri.–Sun. noon–5 p.m.

ARAMENTA CELLARS
17979 NE Lewis Rogers Lane, Newberg
(503) 538 7230
www.aramentacellars.com
Hours: Daily 10:30 a.m.–5 p.m.

ARBORBROOK VINEYARDS
17770 NE Calkins Lane, Newberg
(503) 538 0959
www.arborbrookwines.com
Hours: By appointment

ARCHERY SUMMIT
18599 NE Archery Summit Road,
Dayton
(503) 864 4300
www.archerysummit.com
Hours: Daily 10 a.m.–4:30 p.m.
Tours at 10:30 a.m., 1 p.m. and 3 p.m.
by appointment

ARGYLE WINERY
691 N Highway 99W, Dundee
(503) 538 8520
www.argylewinery.com
Hours: Daily 11 a.m.–5 p.m. Closed
Easter, Thanksgiving, Christmas and
New Year's Day

AUGUST CELLARS
14000 NE Quarry Road, Newberg
(503) 554 6766
www.augustcellars.com
Hours: May–Sep., daily 11 a.m.–5 p.m.;
Oct.–Apr., Fri.–Sun. or by appointment

AYOUB VINEYARD
9650 NE Keyes Lane, Dundee
(503) 554 9583
www.ayoubwines.com
Hours: By appointment, call for
directions

AYRES VINEYARD
17971 NE Lewis Rogers lane, Newberg
(503) 538 7450
www.ayresvineyard.com
Hours: By appointment

BEAUX FRÈRES
15155 NE North Valley Road, Newberg
(503) 537 1137
www.beauxfreres.com
Hours: By appointment

BELLA VIDA VINEYARD
9380 NE Worden Hill Road, Dundee
(503) 538 9821
www.bellavida.com
Hours: Jun.–Nov., Fri.–Sun. 11 a.m.–
5 p.m.

BELLE PENTE WINE CELLARS
12470 NE Rowland Road, Carlton
(503) 852 9500
www.bellepente.com
Hours: By appointment

BERAN VINEYARDS INC.
30088 SW Egger Road, Hillsboro
(503) 628 1298
www.beranvineyards.com
Hours: Apr.–Dec., weekends only
11 a.m.–5 p.m. or by appointment

BERGSTRÖM WINES
18405 NE Calkins Lane, Newberg
(503) 554 0468
www.bergstromwines.com
Hours: Memorial Day and
Thanksgiving weekends or by
appointment

BETHEL HEIGHTS VINEYARD
6060 Bethel Heights Road NW, Salem
(503) 581 2262
www.bethelheights.com
Hours: Jun.–Aug., Tue.–Sun., 11 a.m.–
5 p.m.; Mar.–May and Sep.–Nov.,
weekends only 11 a.m.–5 p.m. Closed
Dec.–Feb. except by appointment

BRICK HOUSE WINE COMPANY
18200 Lewis Rogers Lane, Newberg
(503) 538 5136
www.brickhousewines.com
Hours: By appointment

BOEDECKER CELLARS
At Carlton Winemakers Studio,
Carlton
(503) 288 7752
www.boedeckercellars.com
Hours: Open daily 11 a.m.–5 p.m. Tours
on Sat. noon and 3 p.m. Closed Jan.

BROOKS WINES/THE MORNE WINE
CO.
19143 NE Laughlin Road, Yamhill
(503) 435 1278
Hours: Call for details

BRYCE VINEYARD
At Carlton Winemakers Studio,
Carlton
(503) 852 6100
www.brycevineyard.com
Hours: Daily 11 a.m.–5 p.m.

BRYN MAWR VINEYARDS
5955 Bethel Heights Road NW, Salem
(503) 581 4286
www.brynmawrvineyards.com
Hours: Memorial Day–Thanksgiving,
weekends noon–4 p.m.

CAMERON WINERY
8200 Worden Hill Road, Dundee
(503) 538 0336
www.cameronwines.com
Hours: By appointment

CARABELLA VINEYARD
Edminston Road, Wilsonville
(503) 699 1829
www.carabellawine.com
Hours: Not open to the public

CARLO & JULIAN WINERY
1000 E. Main Street, Carlton
(503) 852 7432
Hours: By appointment

CARLOVANNA VINEYARD
7575 Heron Street NE, Salem
(503) 779 7584
www.carlovanna.com
Hours: By appointment

CARLTON CELLARS
Carlton
(503) 474 8986
www.carltoncellars.com
Hours: Not open to the public

CARLTON HILL WINE CO.
11511 NW Cummins Road, Carlton
(503) 852 7060
www.carltonhillwines.com
Hours: Call for details

CARTER VINEYARD
Eola Hills
(503) 827 4086
www.cartervineyard.com
Hours: Not open to the public

THE CARLTON WINEMAKERS
STUDIO
801 N Scott Street, Carlton
(503) 852 6100
www.winemakersstudio.com
Hours: Open daily 11 a.m.–5 p.m. Tours
on Sat. noon and 3 p.m. Closed Jan.

CHAMPOEG WINE CELLARS
10375 Champoeg Road NE, Aurora
(503) 678 2144
www.champoegwine.com
Hours: Thu.-Mon. 11 a.m.-5 p.m.

CHATEAU BENOIT
Lafayette
1 (800) 248 4835
www.chateaubenoit.com
Hours: Call for details

CHATEAU BIANCA WINERY
17485 Highway 22, Dallas
1 (877) 623 6181
www.chateaubianca.com
Hours: Open daily Jun.-Sep. 10 a.m.-
6 p.m., Oct.-May 11 a.m.-5 p.m.
Closed Jan.

CHEHALEM
31190 NE Veritas Lane, Newberg
(503) 538 4700
www.chehalemwines.com
Hours: Memorial Day and
Thanksgiving weekend or by
appointment

CHERRY HILL WINERY AND GUEST
CAMP
7867 Crowley Road, Rickreall
(503) 623 7867
www.cherryhillwinery.com
Hours: May 1-Oct. 1, weekends 1 p.m.-
5 p.m. Also open Thanksgiving
weekend and by appointment

CHRISTOPHER BRIDGE CELLARS
12770 S Casto Road, Oregon City
(503) 263 6267
www.christopherbridge.net
Hours: Call for details

CLEAR CREEK DISTILLERY
2389 NW Wilson Street, Portland
(503) 248 0490
www.clearcreekdistillery.com
Hours: Call for details

COELHO WINERY
111 Fifth Street, Amity
(503) 835 9305
www.coelhowinery.com
Hours: Jun.-Nov., Fri.-Sun. 11 a.m.-
5 p.m.; Dec.-May, 1st weekend every
month

COEUR DE TERRE VINEYARD
2100 SE Eagle Point Road,
McMinnville
(503) 472 3976
www.cdtvineyard.com
Hours: By appointment

COLEMAN VINEYARD
22734 SW Latham Road, McMinnville
(503) 843 2707
www.colemanvineyard.com
Hours: By appointment

COOPER MOUNTAIN VINEYARDS
WINERY
9480 SW Grabhorn Road, Beaverton
(503) 649 0027
www.coopermountainwine.com
Hours: Feb.-Dec., daily noon-5 p.m.
Jan. by appointment

CRISTOM VINEYARDS
6905 Spring Valley Road NW, Salem
(503) 375 3068
www.cristomwines.com
Hours: Memorial Day-Labor
Day, Wed.-Sun. 11 a.m.-5 p.m.;
April-Memorial Day and Labor
Day-Thanksgiving, Fri. to Sun. 11 a.m.-
5 p.m., or by appointment

CROFT BAILEY VINEYARDS
1301 NE Highway 99W, McMinnville
www.croftbailey.com
Hours: Not open to the public at time
of print

CUBANISIMO VINEYARDS
Salem
(503) 588 1763
www.cubanisimovineyards.com
Hours: Call for details

CUNEO CELLARS
750 Lincoln Street, Carlton
(503) 852 0002
www.cuneocellars.com
Hours: Daily 11 a.m.-5 p.m.

DAEDALUS CELLARS
10505 NE Red Hills Road, Dundee
(503) 537 0727
www.daedaluscellars.com
Hours: Not open to the public

DAVID HILL WINERY
46350 NW David Hill Road, Forest
Grove
(503) 992 8545
www.davidhillwinery.com
Hours: Tue.-Sun. noon-5 p.m.

DE PONTE CELLARS
17545 Archery Summit Road, Dayton
(503) 864 3698
www.depontecellars.com
Hours: By appointment

DIMMICK CELLARS
7401 SW Corbett Avenue, Portland
(503) 246 0659
Hours: By appointment

DOBBES FAMILY ESTATE
240 E 5th Street, Dundee
1 (800) 566 8143
www.dobbesfamilyestate.com
Hours: Daily 11 a.m.-6 p.m.

DOMAINE COTEAU TASTING ROOM
(CARLTON WINE BAR)
258 North Kutch Street, Carlton
(503) 697 7319
www.domainecoteau.com
Hours: Mar.-Nov. weekends noon-5 p.m.

DOMAINE DROUHIN OREGON, INC.
6750 Breyman Orchards Road,
Dundee
(503) 864 2700
www.domainedrouhin.com
Hours: By appointment

DOMAINE MERIWETHER
At Carlton Winemakers Studio,
Carlton
(541) 345 5224
www.meriwetherwines.com
Hours: Daily noon-5 p.m.

DOMAINE SERENE
6555 NE Hilltop Lane, Dayton
(503) 864 4600
www.domaineserene.com
Hours: Thurs.-Sun. 11 a.m.-4 p.m.

DOMINIO IV
At Carlton Winemakers Studio,
Carlton
1 (877) 867 7776
www.dominiowines.com
Hours: Open daily 11 a.m.-5 p.m. Tours
on Sat. noon and 3 p.m. Closed Jan.

DUCK POND CELLARS
23145 Oregon 99W, Dundee
(503) 538 3199
www.duckpondcellars.com
Hours: Open daily; May-Oct.,
10 a.m.-5 p.m.; Nov.-Apr., 11 a.m.-
5 p.m.

DUNDEE SPRINGS WINERY / PERRY
BOWER VINEYARD
Corner Highway 99W and Fox Farm
Road, Dundee
(503) 554 8000
Hours: Call for details

DUSKY GOOSE
Dundee
www.duskygoose.com
Hours: Not open to the public

EIEIO & COMPANY
Carlton
(503) 852 6733
www.OnHisFarm.com
Hours: Taste at Carlton Winemakers
studio

ELK COVE VINEYARDS
27751 NW Olson Road, Gaston
(503) 985 7760
www.elkcove.com
Hours: Daily 10 a.m.–5 p.m.

ELKHORN RIDGE VINEYARDS &
WINERY
10895 Brateng Road, Monmouth
(208) 622 5305
www.elkhornridgevineyards.com
Hours: By appointment, call for details

ELLE REVE WINERY
At August Cellars, Newberg
(503) 538 4662
Hours: May–Sep., daily 11 a.m.–
5 p.m.; Oct.–Apr., weekends only or
by appointment

ELVENGLADE WINERY
Gaston
(503) 662 9960
www.elvenglade.com
Hours: By appointment

ENGELHARDT FARM
10114 Mt Angel-Gervais Road NE, Mt
Angel
(503) 792 4405
Hours: Call for hours

EOLA HILLS WINE CELLARS
501 S Pacific Highway 99 W, Rickreall
(503) 623 2405
www.eolahillswinery.com
Hours: Daily 10 a.m.–5 p.m. Closed
Thanksgiving, Christmas and New
Year's Day

ERATH VINEYARDS
9409 NE Worden Hill Road, Dundee
(503) 538 3318
www.erath.com
Hours: Daily 11 a.m.–5 p.m. Tours by
appointment

ET FILLE WINES INC
At August Cellars, Newberg
(503) 449 5030
www.etfillewines.com
Hours: May–Sep., daily 11 a.m.–5 p.m.;
Oct.–Apr., weekends only or by
appointment

EVESHAM WOOD WINERY
3795 Wallace Road NW, Salem
(503) 371 8478
www.eveshamwood.com
Hours: By appointment

EYRIE VINEYARDS
935 NE 10th Street, McMinnville
(503) 472 5124
www.eyrievineyards.com
Hours: Memorial and Thanksgiving
weekends or by appointment

FERRARO CELLAR
28005 NE Bell Rd, Newberg
(503) 645 0627
www.ferrarocellar.com
Hours: By appointment

FIRESTEED CELLARS
2200 North Pacific Highway West,
Rickreall
(503) 623 8683
www.firesteed.com
Hours: Daily 11 a.m.–5 p.m. Closed
major holidays

FRANCIS TANNAHILL
9360 Eola Hills Road, Amity
(503) 554 1918
www.francistannahill.com
Hours: By appointment

FREJA CELLARS
16691 SW McFee Place, Hillsboro
(503) 628 7843
www.frejacellars.com
Hours: By appointment

GROCHAU CELLARS
17979 NE Lewis Rogers Lane, Newberg
(503) 522 2455
www.gcwines.com
Hours: Call for details

GYPSY DANCER ESTATES
35040 SW Unger Road, Cornelius
(503) 628 0955
www.gypsydancerestates.com
Hours: Not open to the public

HAMACHER WINES
801 N Scott Street, Carlton
(503) 803 6073
www.hamacherwines.com
Hours: Daily 11 a.m.–5 p.m.

HATCHER
9360 Eola Hills Road, Amity
(503) 554 1918
www.hatcherwineworks.com
Hours: By appointment

HAUER OF THE DAUEN WINERY
16425 SE Webfoot Road, Dayton
(503) 868 7359
Hours: Weekends noon–5 p.m. or
by appointment. Closed Easter,
Thanksgiving and Christmas Day

HELVETIA WINERY
22485 NW Yungen Road, Hillsboro
(503) 647 7596
www.helvetiawinery.com
Hours: Weekends noon–5 p.m.

HIP CHICKS DO WINE
4510 SE 23rd, Portland
(503) 234 3790
www.hipchicksdowine.com
Hours: Tue.–Sun. 11 a.m.–6 p.m.

HOLLORAN VINEYARD WINES
2636 SW Schaeffer Road, West Linn
(503) 638 6224
www.holloranvineyardwines.com
Hours: By appointment only except
Memorial Day and Thanksgiving
weekends

HONEYWOOD WINERY
1350 Hines Street SE, Salem
(503) 362 4111
www.honeywoodwinery.com
Hours: Weekdays 9 a.m.–5 p.m., Sat.
10 a.m.–5 p.m., Sun. 1 p.m.–5 p.m.
Closed Easter, Thanksgiving and
Christmas Day

HOUSTON VINEYARDS
86187 Hoya Lane, Eugene
(541) 747 4681
www.HoustonVineyards.com
Hours: By appointment

J. ALBIN WINERY
19495 Vista Hill, Hillsboro
(503) 628 2986
www.jalbinwinery.com
Hours: Special events only

J.K. CARRIERE WINERY
30205 Benjamin Road (just north off
Highway 99W), Newberg
(503) 554 0721
www.jkcarriere.com
Hours: May–Sep., weekends noon–
4 p.m.

J. CHRISTOPHER WINES
2636 SW Schaeffer Road, West Linn
(503) 231 5094
www.jchristopherwines.com
Hours: Call for details (not open to the
public at time of print)

J. DAAN WINE CELLARS
Carlton Winemakers Studio, Carlton
www.jdaan.com
Hours: Open daily 11 a.m.-5 p.m. Tours
on Sat. noon and 3 p.m. Closed Jan.

KATHKEN VINEYARDS
5739 Orchard Heights Road, Salem
(503) 316 3911
kathkenvineyards.com
Hours: Memorial Day-Labor Day,
weekends noon-5 p.m.

KELLEY FAMILY VINEYARDS
18840 Williamson Road, Newberg
(503) 554 8872
Hours: Special events only

KEN WRIGHT CELLARS
236 N Kutch Street, Carlton
(503) 852 7070
www.kenwrightcellars.com
Hours: Not open to the public

KRAMER VINEYARDS
26830 NW Olson Road, Gaston
(503) 662 4545
www.kramerwine.com
Hours: May-Oct. daily, Nov.-Apr.
weekends only. Hours noon-5 p.m.
Closed Jan.-Feb., Easter, Thanksgiving
and New Year's Day

KRISTIN HILL WINERY
3330 SE Amity Dayton Highway,
Amity
(503) 835 0850
Hours: Mar.-Dec. daily noon-5 p.m.;
Jan.-Feb. weekends noon-5 p.m. or by
appointment

LA BÊTE WINES
845 NE 5th Street Suite 400,
McMinnville
(503) 977 1493
www.labetewines.com
Hours: By appointment

LA BONNE TERRE
30875 SW Heater Road, Sherwood
(503) 625 2590
Hours: Call for details

LACHINI VINEYARDS
18225 Calkins Lane, Newburg
(503) 864 4553
www.lachinivineyards.com
Hours: By appointment

LANGE WINERY
18380 NE Buena Vista Drive, Dundee
(503) 538 6476
www.langewinery.com
Hours: Daily 11 a.m.-5 p.m.

LAURA VOLKMAN VINEYARDS
14000 NE Quarry Road, Newberg
(503) 806 4047
www.volkmancellars.com
Hours: By appointment

LAUREL RIDGE WINERY
13301 NE Kuehne Road, Carlton
(503) 852 7050
www.laurelridgewines.com
Hours: Daily 11 a.m.-5 p.m. Closed
major holidays

LAWTON WINERY
20990 NE Kings Grade, Newberg
(503) 538 6509
www.lawtonwinery.com
Hours: Memorial Day and
Thanksgiving weekends or by
appointment

LAZY RIVER VINEYARD
Carlton Winemakers Studio, Carlton
(503) 852 6100
www.lazyrivervineyard.com
Hours: Open daily 11 a.m.-5 p.m. Tours
on Sat. noon and 3 p.m. Closed Jan.

LE CADEAU
Parrett Mountain, Newberg
(503) 625 2777
www.lecadeauvineyard.com
Hours: By appointment

LEMELSON VINEYARDS
12020 NE Stag Hollow Road, Carlton
(503) 852 6619
www.lemelsonvineyards.com
Hours: By appointment

LEWMAN VINEYARD
PO Box 2744, Salem
(503) 365 8859
www.lewmanvineyard.com
Hours: Call for details

MACCALLUM FAMILY CELLARS
Carlton
(503) 345 9218
www.maccallumwines.com
Hours: Not open to the public

MARESH RED BARN
9325 NE Worden Hill Road, Dundee
(503) 538 7034
www.vineyardretreat.com
Hours: Mar.-Thanksgiving, Fri.-Sun.
11 a.m.-5 p.m. or by appointment

MARQUAM HILL VINEYARDS
WINERY
35803 S Highway 213, Molalla
(503) 829 6677
www.marquamhillvineyards.biz
Hours: Open daily (except Mon.);
summer 10 a.m.-6 p.m.; winter
10 a.m.-5 p.m.

MAYSARA ESTATE WINERY
15765 Muddy Valley Road,
McMinnville
(503) 843 1234
www.maysara.com
Hours: Tue.-Sat. noon-6 p.m.

MCKINLAY VINEYARDS
7120 Earlwood Road, Newberg
(503) 625 2534
Hours: Call for details

MEDICI VINEYARDS/WINERY
Newberg
(503) 538 9668
Hours: Call for details

MEKINZIE RIDGE
4733 NE 103rd Avenue, Portland
(503) 760 4757
www.mekinzieridge.com
Hours: Call for details

METHVEN FAMILY WINES
10830 SE Westland Lane, Dayton
(503) 580 1320
www.methvenfamilywines.com
Hours: Daily 8 a.m.-5p.m.

MIA JOVÉ CELLARS
19200 NE Calkins Lane, Newberg
(503) 537 0750
www.miajovecellars.com
Hours: Call for details

MIA SONATINA CELLARS
Tualatin
(503) 449 0834
www.miasonatina.com
Hours: Virtual winery at time of print,
call for current details

MONKS GATE
9500 NE Oak Springs Farm Road,
Carlton
(503) 852 6521
www.monksgate.com
Hours: Call for details

MONTINORE ESTATE
3663 SW Dilley Road, Forest Grove
(503) 359 5012
www.montinore.com
Hours: Mon.-Fri. 11 a.m.-4 p.m.,
weekends 11 a.m.-5 p.m.

MYSTIC WINES
3995 Deepwood Lane NW, Salem
(503) 581 2769
www.mysticwine.com
Hours: May-Nov., weekends only
noon-5 p.m. or by appointment

NAMASTÉ VINEYARDS
5600 Van Well Road, Dallas
(503) 623 4150
www.namastevineyards.com
Hours: Memorial Day-Labor Day,
daily noon-6 p.m., Oct.-Dec. and
Mar.-May, weekends only noon-
6 p.m.; or by appointment

NATALIE'S ESTATE WINERY
16825 NE Chehalem Drive, Newberg
(503) 554 9350
www.nataliesestatewinery.com
Hours: By appointment

NYSA VINEYARD
Dundee
(503) 538 3604
Hours: Call for details

OAK KNOLL WINERY
29700 SW Burkhalter Road, Hillsboro
(503) 648 8198
www.oakknollwinery.com
Hours: Weekdays 11 a.m.-6 p.m.
(5 p.m. during winter), weekends
11 a.m.-5 p.m.

OAK GROVE ORCHARDS WINERY
6090 Crowley Road, Rickreall
(503) 364 7052
Hours: Call for details

ORCHARD HEIGHTS WINERY
6057 Orchard Heights Road NW,
Salem
(503) 391 7308
www.orchardheightswinery.com
Hours: Daily 11 a.m.-5 p.m. Closed
Christmas, Thanksgiving and New
Year's Day

OREGON CASCADE WINERY
20046 S Redland Road, Oregon City
(503) 631 8426
Hours: Call for details

OREGON WINE TASTING ROOM
19690 SW Highway 18, McMinnville
(503) 843 3787
Hours: Daily 11 a.m.-6 p.m.

OSWEGO HILLS
450 S Rosemont Road, West Linn
(503) 655 2599
www.oswegohills.com
Hours: Sun. noon-5 p.m.

OWEN ROE
31590 NE Schaad Road, Newberg
(503) 678 6514
www.owenroe.com
Hours: By appointment

PANTHER CREEK CELLARS
455 N Irvine, McMinnville
(503) 472 8080
www.panthercreekcellars.com
Hours: 2nd Sat. of each month,
Memorial Day and Thanksgiving
weekends or by appointment

PARADIS VINEYARDS
17235 Abiqua Road, Silverton
(503) 873 8475
www.paradiswine.com
Hours: Memorial and Thanksgiving
weekends. Also every 2nd Sat. and by
appointment. Call for details.

PATRICIA GREEN CELLARS
15225 NE North Valley Road, Newberg
(503) 554 0821
www.patriciagreencellars.com
Hours: By appointment

PATTON VALLEY VINEYARD
9449 SW Old Highway 47, PO Box
328, Gaston
(503) 985 3445
www.pattonvalley.com
Hours: By appointment

PENNER-ASH WINE CELLARS
15771 NE Ribbon Ridge Road, Newberg
(503) 554 5545
www.pennerash.com
Hours: Fri.-Sun. 11 a.m.-5 p.m.

PONZI VINEYARDS
14665 SW Winery Lane, Beaverton
(503) 628 1227
www.ponziwines.com
Hours: Daily 11 a.m.-5 p.m.

PRIVÉ VINEYARD & WINERY
28155 NE Bell Road, Newberg
(503) 554 0464
www.privevineyard.com
Hours: By appointment

R. STUART & CO.
845 NE Fifth Street, McMinnville
(503) 472 6990
www.rstuartandco.com
Hours: May-Oct., Mon.-Sat.;
Nov.-Apr. Mon.-Fri. Hours 11 a.m.-
5 p.m. or by appointment

RAPTOR RIDGE WINERY
29090 SW Wildhaven Lane, Hillsboro
(503) 887 5595
www.raptorridge.com
Hours: By appointment

REDHAWK VINEYARD
2995 Michigan City Lane NW, Salem
(503) 362 1596
www.redhawkwine.com
Hours: Apr.-Nov., daily noon-5 p.m.;
Dec.-Mar., Mon.-Fri. noon-5 p.m.

REDMAN VINEYARD AND WINERY
18975 NE Ribbon Ridge Road,
Newberg
(503) 554 1290
www.redmanwines.com
Hours: By appointment

REX HILL VINEYARDS
30835 N Highway 99W, Newberg
1 (800) 739 4455
www.rexhill.com
Hours: Daily 11 a.m.-5 p.m. (Opens
10 a.m. on weekends during summer)

RIBBON RIDGE VINEYARD
At Carlton Winemakers Studio,
Carlton
(503) 502 5255
www.ribbonridge.com
Hours: Open daily 11 a.m.-5 p.m. Tours
on Sat. noon and 3 p.m. Closed Jan.

ROCKBLOCK CELLARS
At Domaine Serene, Dayton
(503) 864 4600
www.rockblocksyrah.com
Hours: Apr.-Nov., Thu.-Sun. 11 a.m.-
4 p.m. or by appointment

SAKÉ ONE
820 Elm Street, Forest Grove
(503) 357 7056
www.sakeone.com
Hours: Daily noon-5 p.m. Tours begin
at 1 p.m., 2 p.m. and 3 p.m.

SALEM HILLS VINEYARD
7934 Skyline Road South, Salem
(503) 362 5250
Hours: Call for details

SASS WINERY
9092 Jackson Hill Road, Salem
(503) 391 9991
Hours: By appointment

SCOTT PAUL WINES
128 S Pine Street, Carlton
(503) 852 7300
www.scottpaul.com
Hours: Wed.-Sun. 11 a.m.-4 p.m. or
by appointment

SEUFERT WINERY
22734 SW Latham Road, McMinnville
(503) 709 1255
www.seufertwinery.com
Hours: By appointment

SHAFER VINEYARD CELLARS
6200 NW Gales Creek Road
Forest Grove
(503) 357 6604
www.shafervineyardcellars.com
Hours: Feb.-Dec., daily 11 a.m.-5 p.m.;
Jan., weekends only 11 a.m.-5 p.m.

SHEA WINE CELLARS
4304 SW Strathfell Lane, Portland
(503) 241 6527
www.sheawinecellars.com
Hours: Not open to the public

SILVER FALLS VINEYARDS
4972 Cascade Highway SE, Sublimity
(503) 769 5056
www.silverfallsvineyards.com
Hours: Weekends and by appointment

SINEANN CELLARS
28005 NE Bell Road, Newberg
(503) 341 2698
www.sineann.com
Hours: By appointment

SOKOL BLOSSER WINERY
5000 Sokol Blosser Lane, Dundee
1 (800) 582 6668
www.sokolblosser.com
Hours: Daily 11 a.m.-5 p.m.

SOLENA CELLARS
213 Pine Street, Carlton
(503) 852 0082
www.solenacellars.com
Hours: Thu.-Sun. noon-5 p.m.

SOTER VINEYARDS
Yamhill
(503) 662 5600
www.sotervineyards.com
Hours: By appointment

ST. INNOCENT WINERY
1360 Tandem Avenue NE, Salem
(503) 378 1526
www.stinnocentwine.com
Hours: Weekends noon-5 p.m. or by
appointment

ST. JOSEF'S WINE CELLAR
28836 S Barlow Road, Canby
(503) 651 3190
Hours: May-Sep., Thu.-Mon. noon-
5 p.m.; Oct.-Apr., weekends noon-
5 p.m.; or by appointment

STAG HOLLOW
7930 NE Blackburn Road, Yamhill
(503) 662 5609
www.staghollow.com
Hours: By appointment

STANGELAND WINERY
8500 Hopewell Road NW, Salem
(503) 581 0355
www.stangelandwinery.com
Hours: Jun.-Nov., weekends noon-
5 p.m.; Dec.-May, first weekend of
each month. Also holiday weekends
and by appointment

STOLLER VINEYARDS
16161 NE McDougall Road, Dayton
(503) 864 3404
www.stollervineyards.com
Hours: By appointment

STONE WOLF VINEYARDS
2155 NE Lafayette Avenue,
McMinnville
(503) 434 9025
www.stonewolfvineyards.com
Hours: Call for details

STONY MOUNTAIN VINEYARD
27734 SW Latham Road, McMinnville
(503) 550 6317
Hours: By appointment

STYRING VINEYARDS
19960 NE Ribbon Ridge Road,
Newberg
(503) 866 6741
www.styringvineyards.com
Hours: Call for details

TEMPTRESS WINES
2517 NW 83rd Place, Portland
(503) 730 9633
www.temptresswines.com
Hours: Not open to the public

THE TRADITIONAL COMPANY
6130 Bethel Heights Road NW, Salem
(503) 361 2410
www.traditionalcompany.com
Hours: By appointment

THISTLE WINES (AT KRAMER
VINEYARDS)
26830 NW Olson Road, Gaston
(503) 590 0449
www.thistlewines.com
Hours: By appointment

TORII MOR WINERY (TASTING
ROOM)
18325 NE Fairview Drive, Dundee
(503) 538 2279
www.toriimorwinery.com
Hours: Daily 11 a.m.-5 p.m.
Closed Tue.

TUALATIN ESTATE VINEYARDS
10850 NE Seavy Road, Forest Grove
(503) 357 5005
www.tualatinestate.com
Hours: Mar. 1-Dec. 31, weekends
noon-5 p.m. or by appointment

TWELVE
Carlton
(503) 358 6707
www.twelvewine.com
Hours: Not open to the public

TYRUS EVAN
120 N Pine Street (The Depot),
Carlton
(503) 852 7070
www.tyrusevan.com
Hours: Call for details

URBAN WINEWORKS/BISHOP
CREEK CELLARS
407 NW 16th Avenue (16th and
Flanders), Portland
(503) 226 9797
www.urbanwineworks.com
Hours: Mon.-Sat. noon-8:30 p.m.,
Sun. noon-6 p.m.

VAN DUZER VINEYARDS
11975 Smithfield Road, Dallas
(503) 623 6420
www.vanduzer.com
Hours: Mar. 1-Dec. 30, daily 11 a.m.-
5 p.m.; by appointment during
Jan.-Feb.

VIDON VINEYARD
17425 NE Hillside Drive, Newberg
(503) 538 4092
www.vidonvineyard.com
Hours: By appointment only

VITIS RIDGE
6685 Meridian Road NE, Silverton
(503) 873 8304
www.vitisridge.com
Hours: 2nd weekend of each month
noon-5 p.m.

WALNUT CITY WINEWORKS
475 NE 17th (at Evans), McMinnville
(503) 472 3215
www.walnutcitywineworks.com
Hours: Thu.-Sun. 11 a.m.-4:30 p.m.

WESTREY WINE CO.
1065 NE Alpine Avenue, McMinnville
(503) 434 6357
www.westrey.com
Hours: By appointment

WHITE ROSE WINES
6250 NE Hilltop Lane, Dayton
(949) 275 8021
www.whiterosewines.com
Hours: Daily 11 a.m.-dark

WILLAKENZIE ESTATE
19143 NE Laughlin Road, Yamhill
(503) 662 3280
www.willakenzie.com
Hours: Memorial Day-Labor Day
noon-5 p.m. Rest of year weekends
noon-5 p.m. or by appointment

VERCING ETORIX—WILLAMETTE
FARMS OF OREGON
8000 NE Parrish Road, Newberg
(503) 538 9895
www.willamettefarms.com
Hours: By appointment

WHISTLING RIDGE VINEYARDS
14551 NE North Valley Road, Newberg
(503) 538 6641
www.whistlingridgevineyard.com
Hours: Thanksgiving and Memorial
Day weekends

WILLAMETTE VALLEY VINEYARDS
8800 Enchanted Way SE, Turner
1 (800) 344 9463
www.wvv.com
Hours: Daily 11 a.m.-6 p.m. Call for
tour schedule

WINE COUNTRY FARM CELLARS
6855 Breyman Orchards Road, Dayton
1 (800) 261 3446
www.winecountryfarm.com
Hours: Memorial Day-Thanksgiving,
daily 11 a.m.-5 p.m.; winter, weekends
only 11 a.m.-5 p.m.

WINTER'S HILL VINEYARD
Layfette School House Antique Mall
748 Highway 99W, Lafayette
(503) 864 4610
www.wintershillwine.com
Hours: Weekends 11 a.m.-5 p.m. or by
appointment

WITNESS TREE VINEYARD
7111 Spring Valley Road NW, Salem
(503) 585 7874
www.witnesstreevineyard.com
Hours: Jun.-Aug., Tue.-Sun. 11 a.m.-
5 p.m.; Mar.-May and Sep.-Dec.,
weekends only 11 a.m.-5 p.m.

YAMHILL VALLEY VINEYARDS
16250 SW Oldsville Road,
McMinnville
1 (800) 825 4845
www.yamhill.com
Hours: Memorial Day-Thanksgiving,
daily 11 a.m.-5 p.m.; mid-Mar.-
Memorial Day, weekends only 11 a.m.-
5 p.m. Closed during winter

YOUNGBERG HILL VINEYARDS
10660 SW Youngberg Hill Road,
McMinnville
(503) 472 2727
www.youngberghill.com
Hours: By appointment

ZENAS WINES
7430 Tingley Lane, Klamath Falls
(541) 273 6971
www.zenaswines.com
Hours: By appointment

ZENAS WINES TASTING ROOM
407 W Main #7, Carlton
(503) 852 3000
www.zenaswines.com
Hours: Sat. 1 p.m.-5 p.m.

ZIVO AT WINEWORKS
475 NE 17th Street, McMinnville
(503) 705 9398
Hours: By appointment

Wineries of the South Willamette Valley

720 WINE CELLARS
Philomath
(541) 929 4562
www.720cellars.com
Hours: Not open to the public

ALPINE VINEYARDS
25904 Greek Peak Road, Monroe
(541) 424 5851
Hours: Not open to the public

BELLE VALLÉE CELLARS
Corvallis
(541) 231 7972
www.bellevallee.com
Hours: Call for details

BELLFOUNTAIN CELLARS
24041 Llewellyn Road, Corvallis
(541) 929 3162
Hours: By appointment

BENTON-LANE WINERY
23924 Territorial Road, Monroe
(541) 847 5792
www.benton-lane.com
Hours: Daily from Labor Day-
Thanksgiving

BRIGGS HILL VINEYARDS
27127 Briggs Hill Road, Eugene
(541) 341 3974
www.briggshill.com
Hours: Not open to the public

BROADLEY VINEYARDS
25158 Orchard Tract Road, Monroe
(541) 847 5934
www.broadleyvineyards.com
Hours: By appointment

CHATEAU LORANE WINERY
27415 Siuslaw River Road, Lorane
(541) 942 8028
www.chateaulorane.com
Hours: Jun.-Sep., daily noon-5 p.m.;
Jan.-May and Oct.-Dec., weekends
noon-5 p.m. and by appointment

EUGENE WINE CELLARS
255 Madison Street, Eugene
(541) 342 2600
www.eugenewinecellars.com
Hours: Mon.-Fri. 10 a.m.-4 p.m., Sat.
1 p.m.-7 p.m.

HARRIS BRIDGE VINEYARD
22937 Harris Road, Philomath
(541) 929 3053
www.harrisbridgevineyard.com
Hours: May-Sep., weekends noon-
6 p.m., Also open Thanksgiving
weekend

HIGH PASS WINERY
24757 Lavell Road, Junction City
(541) 998 1447
www.highpasswinery.com
Hours: By appointment

IRIS HILL
82110 Territorial Road (At Iris Hill
Lane), Eugene
(541) 895 9877
www.iris-hill.com
Hours: Memorial Day-Thanksgiving
weekends,Thu.-Sun. noon-5 p.m. or by
appointment

Wineries of the South Willamette Valley

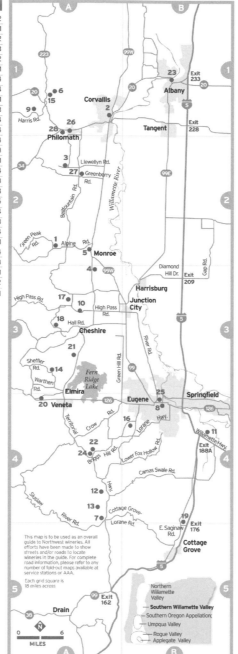

This map is to be used as an overall guide to Northwest wineries. All efforts have been made to show streets and/or roads to locate wineries in the guide. For complete road information, please refer to any number of fold-out maps available at service stations or AAA.

Each grid square is 18 miles across.

MILES

MICHAEL MODE/THE OREGONIAN

Northern Willamette Valley
— Southern Willamette Valley
— Southern Oregon Appellation;
— Umpqua Valley
— Rogue Valley
— Applegate Valley

KING ESTATE WINERY
80854 Territorial Road, Eugene
(541) 942 9874
www.kingestate.com
Hours: Open daily 11 a.m.–6 p.m.

LAVELLE VINEYARDS
89697 Sheffler Road, Elmira
(541) 935 9406
www.lavelle-vineyards.com
Hours: Open daily noon–5 p.m.

LUMOS WINE COMPANY
24000 Cardwell Hill Drive, Philomath
(541) 929 6257
www.lumoswine.com
Hours: Call for details

NOBLE ESTATE VINEYARD
29210 Gimpl Hill Road, Eugene
(541) 954 9870
www.nobleestatevineyard.com
Hours: By appointment

PFEIFFER VINEYARDS
25040 Jaeg Road, Junction City
(541) 998 2828
www.villaevenings.com
Hours: Call for details

PHEASANT COURT WINERY
1301 Main Street, Philomath
(541) 929 8496
www.pheasantcourtwinery.com
Hours: Weekends noon–6 p.m.

RAINSONG WINERY
92989 Goldson/Templeton Road
Chesire
(541) 998 1786
Hours: By appointment

SAGINAW VINEYARD
80247 Delight Valley Road
Cottage Grove
(541) 942 1364
Hours: Wed.–Sun. 11 a.m.–5 p.m.

SECRET HOUSE VINEYARDS
88324 Vineyard Lane, Veneta
(541) 935 3774
www.secrethousewinery.com
Hours: Daily 11 a.m.–5 p.m.

SILVAN RIDGE/HINMAN VINEYARDS
27012 Briggs Hill Road, Eugene
(541) 345 1945
www.silvanridge.com
Hours: Daily noon–5 p.m.

Wineries of the Umpqua, Rogue and Applegate Valleys

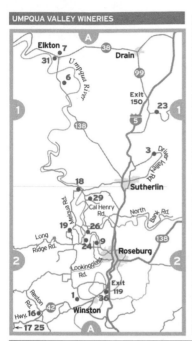

1.	Abacela Winery	A2
2.	Academy of Wine of Oregon Inc.	B3
3.	Amaranth Ridge	A1
4.	Ashland Vineyards and Winery	C3
5.	Bear Creek Winery/Siskiyou Vineyards	A3
6.	Bradley Vineyards	A1
7.	Brandborg Vineyard & Winery	A1
8.	Bridgeview Vineyards	A3, B3
9.	Champagne Creek Cellars	A2
10.	Cliff Creek	B3
11.	Crater Lake Cellars	B3
12.	Del Rio Vineyards	B3
13.	Devitt Winery	B3
14.	EdenVale Estate Winery at Eden Valley Orchards	B3
15.	Foris Vineyards Winery	A3
16.	Girardet Wine Cellars	A2
17.	Hawks View Winery	A2
18.	Henry Estate Winery	A2
19.	HillCrest Vineyard	A2
20.	Jacksonville Vineyard & Winery	B3
21.	John Michael Champagne Cellars	B3
22.	LongSword Vineyard	B3
23.	MarshAnne Landing	A1
24.	Melrose Vineyard	A2
25.	Old Bridge Winery	A2
26.	Palotai Vineyard & Winery	A2
27.	Paschal Winery & Vineyard	B3

28.	Pheasant Hill Vineyards	B3
29.	Reustle-Prayer Rock Vineyards	A2
30.	Rising Sun Farms	B3
31.	River's Edge Winery	A1
32.	Rogue Valley Wine Center at Eden Valley Orchards	B3
33.	Rosella's Vineyard and Winery	B3
34.	RoxyAnn Winery	B3
35.	Schmidt Family Vineyards	B3
36.	Spangler Vineyards	A2
37.	Trium Vineyards	B3
38.	Troon Vineyard	B3
39.	Valley View Winery	B3
40.	Velocity Cellars	B3
41.	Weisinger's of Ashland Winery	C3
42.	Wooldridge Creek Winery	B3

Northern Willamette Valley

Southern Willamette Valley

Southern Oregon Appellation:
Umpqua Valley
Rogue Valley
Applegate Valley

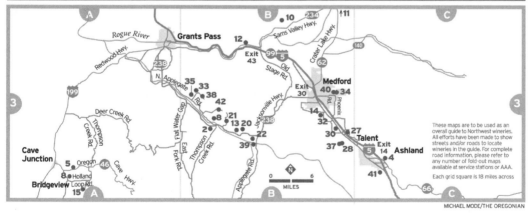

These maps are to be used as an overall guide to Northwest wineries. All efforts have been made to show streets and/or roads to locate wineries in the guide. For complete road information, please refer to any number of fold-out maps available at service stations or AAA.

Each grid square is 18 miles across

MICHAEL MODE/THE OREGONIAN

SPINDRIFT CELLARS
810 Applegate Street, Philomath
(541) 929 6555
www.spindriftcellars.com
Hours: Weekends 1 p.m.–5 p.m.

SPRINGHILL CELLARS
2920 NW Scenic Drive, Albany
(541) 928 1009
www.springhillcellars.com
Hours: By appointment

SWEET CHEEKS WINERY
26961 Briggs Hill Road, Eugene
(541) 349 9463
www.sweetcheekswinery.com
Hours: Daily noon–6 p.m.,
Fri. until 9 p.m.

TERRITORIAL VINEYARDS & WINE
COMPANY
907 West 3rd Avenue, Eugene
(541) 684 9463
www.territorialvineyards.com
Hours: Thu. 5 p.m.–11 p.m., Fri.-Sat.
2 p.m.–7 p.m. or by appointment

THE WINE VAULT
1301 Main Street, Philomath
(541) 929 8496
www.winevault.biz
Hours: Weekends noon–6 p.m.

TYEE WINE CELLARS
26335 Greenberry Road, Corvallis
(541) 753 8754
www.tyeewine.com
Hours: June 15–Labor day, open daily
noon–5 p.m.; all other times weekends
only noon–5 p.m.; or by appointment

Wineries of the Umpqua, Rogue and Applegate Valleys

ABACELA WINERY
12500 Lookingglass Road, Roseburg
(541) 679 6642
www.abacela.com
Hours: Daily 11 a.m.–5 p.m.

AMARANTH RIDGE
5500 Driver Valley Road, Oakland
www.amaranthridge.com
Hours: Call for details

ACADEMY OF WINE OF OREGON
INC.
18200 Highway 238 (Applegate, mile
marker 18), Grants Pass
(541) 846 6817
Hours: By appointment and most
holiday weekends

ASHLAND VINEYARDS
2775 E. Main Street, Ashland
(541) 488 0088
www.winenet.com
Hours: Tue.-Sun. 11 a.m.–5 p.m.

BEAR CREEK WINERY / SISKIYOU
VINEYARDS
6220 Caves Highway, Cave Junction
(541) 592 3977
www.sv-wine.com
Hours: Memorial Day–Labor Day,
daily noon–5 p.m.; otherwise by
appointment

BRADLEY VINEYARDS
2353 Azalea Drive, Elkton
(541) 584 2464
Hours: Call for details

BRANDBORG VINEYARD AND
WINERY
345 First Street, Elkton
(541) 584 2870
www.brandborgwine.com
Hours: Memorial Day–Labor Day,
daily 11 a.m.–5 p.m.; Oct.-Dec.
and Mar.-May, weekends only
11 a.m.–5 p.m.

BRIDGEVIEW VINEYARDS & WINERY
4210 Holland Loop Road, Cave
Junction
(541) 592 4688
www.bridgeviewwine.com
Hours: Daily 11 a.m.–5 p.m.

CHAMPAGNE CREEK CELLARS
340 Busenbark Lane, Roseburg
(541) 673 7901
www.champagnecreek.com
Hours: Daily 11 a.m. to 5 p.m.
(6 p.m. summer)

CLIFF CREEK
1015 McDonough Road, Gold Hill
(541) 855 9819
www.cliffcreek.com
Hours: Not open to the public

DEL RIO VINEYARDS
52 N River Road, Gold Hill
(541) 855 2062
www.delriovineyards.com
Hours: Daily 11 a.m.–5 p.m. (6 p.m.
during summer)

DENINO UMPQUA RIVER ESTATE
451 Hess Lane, Roseburg
(541) 673 1975
Hours: Call for details

DEVITT WINERY
11412 Highway 238, Jacksonville
(541) 899 7511
www.devittwinery.com
Hours: Call for details

EDENVALE WINERY
2310 Voorhies Road, Medford
(541) 512 2955
www.edenvalewines.com
Hours: Mon.-Sat. 10 a.m.–6 p.m.
(5 p.m. during winter), Sun. noon–
4 p.m.; closed Mon. during winter.

FORIS VINEYARDS WINERY
654 Kendall Road, Cave Junction
1 (800) 843 6747
www.foriswine.com
Hours: Daily 11 a.m.–5 p.m.

GIRARDET WINE CELLARS
895 Reston Road, Roseburg
(541) 679 7252
www.girardetwine.com
Hours: Daily 11 a.m.–5 p.m. Closed
major holidays

GRANITE PEAK
Umpqua
(541) 840 0299
Hours: Not open to the public

HENRY ESTATE WINERY
687 Hubbard Creek Road, Umpqua
(541) 459 5120
www.henryestate.com
Hours: Daily 11 a.m.–5 p.m.

HILLCREST VINEYARD
240 Vineyard Lane, Roseburg
(541) 673 3709
www.hillcrestvineyard.com
Hours: Daily 11 a.m.–5 p.m.

JACKSONVILLE VINEYARDS
9730 Highway.238, Jacksonville
(541) 899 6923
www.jacksonvillevineyards.com
Hours: Call for details

JOHN MICHAEL'S CHAMPAGNE
CELLAR
1425 Humbug Creek Road, Applegate
(541) 846 6400
Hours: By appointment

LONGSWORD VINEYARD
8555 Highway 238, Jacksonville
(541) 899 1746
www.longswordvineyard.com
Hours: May-Oct, daily 11 a.m.-5 p.m.,
Nov.-Apr. weekends at Fiasco Winery

MADRONE MOUNTAIN
540 Tumbleweed Trail, Jacksonville
(541) 899 9642
www.madronemountain.com
Hours: Call for details

MARSHANNE LANDING
381 Hogan Road, Oakland
(541) 459 8497
www.marshannelanding.com
Hours: Memorial Day-Labor Day and
Thanksgiving-Christmas, weekends
11 a.m.-5 p.m.; other times by
appointment

MELROSE VINEYARDS
885 Melqua Road, Roseburg
(541) 672 6080
www.melrosevineyards.com
Hours: Daily 11 a.m.-5 p.m.; Jan.-Mar.,
by appointment only

OLD BRIDGE WINERY
50706 Sandy Creek Road, Remote
(541) 572 0272
Hours: Daily 11 a.m.-5 p.m.
Closed Mon.

PALOTAI VINEYARD AND WINERY
272 Capital Lane, Roseburg
(541) 464 0032
Hours: Apr.-Dec, Fri.-Sun.
11 a.m.-5 p.m.

PASCHAL WINERY
1122 Suncrest Road, Talent
(541) 535 7957
www.paschalwinery.com
Hours: Summer, daily 11 a.m.-6 p.m.;
winter, Tue.-Sun. 11 a.m.-5 p.m.

REUSTLE PRAYER ROCK VINEYARDS
960 Cal Henry Road, Roseburg
(541) 459 6060
www.reustlevineyards.com
Hours: Mon.-Sat. 11 a.m.-5 p.m.

RISING SUN FARMS
5126 South Pacific Highway, Phoenix
(541) 535 8331
www.risingsunfarms.com
Hours: Daily 10 a.m.-5 p.m.

RIVER'S EDGE WINERY
1395 River Drive, Elkton
(541) 584 2357
www.riversedgewinery.com
Hours: Summer, daily 11 a.m.-5 p.m.;
end of summer-Nov., Wed.-Sun.
11 a.m.-5 p.m.; otherwise by
appointment

ROSELLA'S VINEYARD & WINERY
184 Missouri Flat Road, Grants Pass
(541) 846 6372
www.rosellasvineyard.com
Hours: Thu.-Mon. 11 a.m.-5 p.m. or by
appointment

ROXYANN WINERY
3285 Hillcrest Road, Medford
(541) 776 2315
www.roxyann.com
Hours: Open daily 11 a.m.-6 p.m.

CRATER LAKE CELLARS
21882 Highway 62 Bldg B, Shady Cove
(541) 878 4200
Hours: Daily 11 a.m.-5 p.m.

SCHMIDT FAMILY VINEYARD
242 Missouri Flat Road, Applegate
(541) 846 9985
Hours: Not open to the public

SPANGLER VINEYARDS (LA GARZA
CELLARS)
491 Winery Lane, Roseburg
(541) 679 9654
www.spanglervineyards.com
Hours: Daily 11 a.m.-5 p.m.

TRIUM WINE
7112 Rapp Lane, Talent
(541) 535 4015
www.triumwine.com
Hours: By appointment

TROON VINEYARD
1475 Kubli Road, Grants Pass
(541) 846 9900
www.troonvineyard.com
Hours: Open daily 11 a.m.-6 p.m. or by
appointment. Closed during Jan.

VALLEY VIEW WINERY
1000 Upper Applegate Road,
Jacksonville
(541) 899 8468
www.valleyviewwinery.com
Hours: Daily 11 a.m.-5 p.m.

VELOCITY WINE CELLARS
2000 Ashland Mine Road, Ashland
(541) 482 9336
www.velocitycellars.com
Hours: Tasting Room is at
Roxy Ann Winery

WEISINGER'S OF ASHLAND WINERY
3150 Siskiyou Blvd, Ashland
(541) 488 5989
www.weisingers.com
Hours: Spring and summer, daily
10 a.m.-6 p.m.; fall and winter,
Wed.-Sun. 11 a.m.-5 p.m.

WETHERELL VINEYARDS
577 Mode Road, Umpqua
(541) 459 4222
Hours: Call for details

WOOLRIDGE CREEK VINEYARD
818 Slagle Creek Road, Grants Pass
(541) 846 6364
www.wcwinery.com
Hours: Open weekends 11 a.m.-5 p.m.,
or by appointment

Wineries of the Columbia River Area

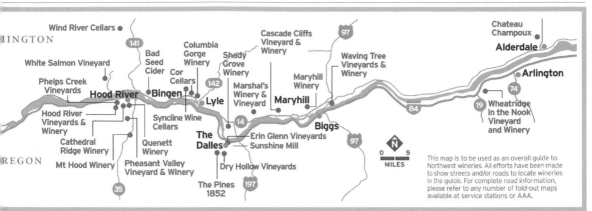

WINERIES OF THE COLUMBIA RIVER AREA

BLUE DOG MEAD COMPANY
1819 E 9th Street, The Dalles
(541) 506 1560
Hours: Call for details

CATHEDRAL RIDGE WINERY
4200 Post Canyon Drive, Hood River
1 (800) 516 8710
www.cathedralridgewinery.com
Hours: Daily 11 a.m.–5 p.m.

DRY HOLLOW VINEYARDS
3410 Dry Hollow Lane, The Dalles
(541) 296 2953
www.dryhollowvineyards.com
Hours: Memorial Day–Thanksgiving,
Fri.–Sun. noon–5 p.m., or by
appointment

EDGEFIELD WINERY
2126 SW Halsey Street, Troutdale
(503) 665 2992
www.mcmenamins.com
Hours: Summer daily noon–10 p.m.;
winter Sun.–Thu. noon–8 p.m., Fri.–Sat.
noon–10 p.m.

ERIN GLENN WINES AT THE MINT
710 East 2nd Street, The Dalles
(541) 296 4707
Hours: Call for hours

HOOD RIVER VINEYARDS
4693 Westwood Drive, Hood River
(541) 386 3772
www.hoodrivervineyards.com
Hours: Daily 11 a.m.–5 p.m.

MOUNT HOOD WINERY
3189 Highway 35, Hood River
(541) 386 8333
www.mthoodwinery.com
Hours: Mid-Apr.–late-Oct., daily
noon–5 p.m.

PHELPS CREEK VINEYARDS
1808 Country Club Road, Hood River
(541) 490 6942
Hours: Open daily 11 a.m.–5 p.m.

PHEASANT VALLEY VINEYARD AND
WINERY
3890 Acree Drive, Hood River
(541) 387 3040
www.pheasantvalleywinery.com
Hours: Summer, daily 11 a.m.–6 p.m.;
winter, daily 11 a.m.–5 p.m.

QUENETT WINERY TASTING ROOM
111 Oak Street (cnr 2nd and Oak),
Hood River
(541) 386 2229
www.quenett.com
Hours: Daily 10 a.m.–6 p.m.

SUNSHINE MILL
901 E 2nd Street, The Dalles
(541) 298 8900
www.sunshinemill.com
Hours: Call for details

THE PINES 1852
5450 Mill Creek Road, The Dalles
(541) 298 1981
www.thepinesvineyard.com
Hours: By appointment

VIENTO WINES, INC.
At Pheasant Valley Winery,
Hood River
(541) 387 3040
www.vientowines.com
Hours: Daily 11 a.m.–6 p.m.

WASSON BROTHERS WINERY
17020 Ruben Lane, Sandy
(503) 668 3124
www.wassonbrotherswinery.com
Hours: Daily 9 a.m.–5 p.m.

WHEATRIDGE IN THE NOOK
WINERY
11102 Philippi Canyon Lane, Arlington
(541) 454 2585
www.wheatridgeinthenook.com
Hours: Daily 11 a.m.–6 p.m.

Wineries of the Pacific Coast and Other Regions

BENDISTILLERY SAMPLE ROOM
850 NW Brooks Street, Bend
(541) 388 6868
www.bendistillery.com
Hours: Mon.-Sat. 4 p.m.–midnight

BRANDY PEAK DISTILLERY
18526 Tetley Road, Brookings
(541) 469 0194
www.brandypeak.com
Hours: Mar.-Jan., Tue.-Sat.
1 p.m–5 p.m.

DAVID HAMILTON WINERY
150 Mountain Blvd, Mt. Vernon
(541) 932 4567
www.davidhamiltonwinery.com
Hours: Call for details

DEPOE BAY WINERY
22 SE Highway 101, Depoe Bay
(541) 765 3311
Hours: Open daily

FLYING DUTCHMAN WINERY
915 First Street, Otter Rock
(541) 765 2553
www.dutchmanwinery.com
Hours: May-Oct., daily 11 a.m.–6 p.m.;
Nov.-Apr. 11 a.m.–5 p.m.

GILSTRAP BROTHERS
69789 Antles Lane, Cove
(541) 568 4646
www.gilstrapbrothers.com
Hours: Call for details

LAUREL HOOD WINES
263 N Hemlock Street, Cannon Beach
(503) 436 1666
Hours: Call for details

MARAGAS WINERY
643 NW Colorado Avenue, Bend
(541) 330 0919
www.maragas.com
Hours: Tue.-Sun. 11:30 a.m.–5:30 p.m.

NEHALEM BAY WINE COMPANY
34965 Highway 53, Nehalem
(503) 368 9463
www.nehalembaywinery.com
Hours: Open daily

SHALLON WINERY
1598 Duane Street, Astoria
(503) 325 5978
www.shallon.com
Hours: Daily 1 p.m.–6 p.m.

VOLCANO VINEYARDS
930 NW Brooks Street, Bend
(541) 617 1102
www.volcanovineyards.com
Hours: Wed.-Sat. noon-6 p.m. Sun.
noon-5 p.m. or by appointment

ZERBA CELLARS
85530 Highway 11, Milton-Freewater
(541) 938 9463
www.zerbacellars.com
Hours: Mon.-Sat. noon-5 p.m. Sun.
noon-4 p.m. or by appointment

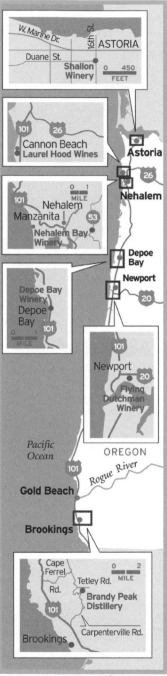

MICHAEL MODE/THE OREGONIAN

SPECIAL THANKS

A special thanks to everyone who went out of their way to help us put this book together. It would not have been possible without your time, advice and generosity. Of special note are Michael Strang, Angela McLean, Elaine Jones and Gavin Forbes. Thank you to our parents for their inspiration, enthusiasm and encouragement. Thanks also to Brent and Sarah for letting us raid their garden. And Blair, we will always miss you.

FURTHER READING

For further reading on the food and wine of the Pacific Northwest two excellent magazines are *Wine Press Northwest* and *Northwest Palate*.

About the Authors

Troy Townsin was born in Melbourne, Australia, and worked as an actor and playwright before embarking on a round-the-world backpacking extravaganza. After establishing a career in hospitality he returned to Melbourne and earned a Bachelor of Arts in International Studies, taking semesters in Malaysia, Turkey and the UK. While studying in Malaysia he met his wife, Cheryl-Lynn. After graduating, he worked for the United Nations Information Centre in London before taking a job as an event reporter. In 2003, he won the prestigious Travel Writer of the Year award with *TNT Magazine UK*. After moving to the Pacific Northwest in 2004, Troy co-authored *Cooking with BC Wine*, a 2005 Gourmand World Cookbook Award winner. In 2006 Troy ran a weekly "Time for Wine" column on CBC radio.

Cheryl-Lynn Townsin was born and raised in British Columbia. She completed her Bachelor of Commerce in International Business at the University of Victoria. Pursuing an international career in business she has worked and traveled extensively throughout South East Asia, Europe and the Middle East. Eventually the lure of the Pacific Northwest proved too much and she returned to be married in 2004. Cheryl-Lynn co-authored *Cooking with BC Wine* and is currently coordinating international programs for Royal Roads University.